Smart Guide for
AWESOME MEMORY

Shireen Stephen

RUPA

Published by
Rupa Publications India Pvt. Ltd 2018
7/16, Ansari Road, Daryaganj
New Delhi 110002

P-ISBN: 978-81-291-5148-3
E-ISBN: 978-81-291-5149-0

Fourth impression 2024

10 9 8 7 6 5 4

To my amazing family,
especially my loving husband Rabin and
my wonderful daughters Shifrah and Annika

Contents

Chapter 1

Introduction to Memory

'On our first day of school in fourth grade, our class teacher asked us to introduce ourselves by telling her our names and hobbies. She listened attentively while all fifty-five of us stood up one at a time and introduced ourselves. Once we were done, she shocked all of us by repeating all our names and hobbies correctly. Throughout that year, she never once used the attendance register, but always knew who was absent!'

Memory is the ability to remember something that happened in the past. You experience many things in your daily life through the five senses of touch, taste, smell, sight and sound. Whatever you retain through your five senses is called memory.

Imagine a world where memory did not exist. You would wake up each morning wondering who you were; you would not know how to button your shirt or how to brush your teeth; you would not know what your favourite food is or what it looks like; you wouldn't know who your friends are or maybe even what friendship is. You would constantly be living in the present but you would not know anything about your past. Every moment would be a fresh experience but even then, you would immediately forget what you did or said just a minute ago!

Now imagine a world where memory was perfect. You would remember every single thing you had ever studied; you would recall everything about the people you met every day—their names, hobbies, birthdays, etc. You would remember that you don't like broccoli, but love chocolate. You would recollect every incident that happened in your life and all your emotions, people and situations that were responsible for them. Indeed, you would never forget anything!

Not many people have a perfect memory, but you can certainly train yourself to develop a memory that is nothing short of amazing! Memory is like a muscle—the more you exercise it, the stronger it becomes. You can use certain memory techniques to strengthen your memory. These techniques can help you remember every formula in chemistry and mathematics, every significant date in history and civics, every poem in English literature and every minute detail of each diagram in biology and physics! You can also use these memory techniques to remember names, addresses, telephone numbers, birthdays and anniversaries.

By taking the time to learn and practise these techniques, you will find a drastic improvement in your concentration, your thinking will become clearer, your observation skills and self-confidence will improve and you will be able to study effectively by using the least amount of effort. These techniques are discussed in the following chapters. However, before moving on, it is important to know about the different types of memory and how these work.

Types of Memory

There are three types of memory depending on for how long the information is stored in your mind. To illustrate this, imagine there's a new boy in class from Africa and your teacher introduces him as Moussa Cooney. Since it is a strange and foreign name to you, it is likely that you may forget it as soon as you hear it. This kind of memory is called **Sensory Memory**, which is fleeting and lasts only for an instant. If your friend sitting next to you asks you what the teacher just said, you would be able to tell the new boy's name. However, if your friend asks you the same question during lunch break, you may have forgotten it. This kind of memory is called **Short-term Memory**, which allows you to store information for a few seconds. If you were to keep repeating the name over and over in your mind or use a memory technique and picture George Clooney holding a mouse every time you saw Moussa Cooney, you may never forget his name. This kind of memory is called **Long-term Memory**, which allows you to store information on a relatively permanent basis.

Long-term memory is further divided into three major types: Semantic Memory, Episodic Memory and Procedural Memory. Do you remember the last mathematics formula that you learnt? Or the last diagram that you drew in biology? This kind of memory is called **Semantic Memory**, which helps you remember facts, figures and concepts. It helps you prepare for exams.

Now, think of the last movie that you watched in the theatre. Do you remember who you went with and what you did that day? This kind of memory is called **Episodic Memory**, which helps you remember 'episodes' or events in your life effortlessly. It helps you remember events such as going to that basketball game last week, what you did on a holiday last summer or the day that you brought your puppy home for the first time.

Procedural Memory comprises skill- and task-based information. This helps you learn to cycle, swim, or play a musical instrument. These skill-based memories strengthen with practice.

You may find it easier to remember the details of the last movie that you watched rather than the formula or diagram. This is because *your brain remembers vividly imagined experiences exactly the same way as real experiences.* It means that if you can visualize and see your study material vividly like a movie in your mind, you will be able to remember even the most difficult information easily.

How Memory Works

Think of your brain like a computer and your mind like the software for your computer. You can program and reprogram your mind any way that you want. To remember any event, you first need to input information into your brain using any of your senses. Your mind then converts it into its own neural language and stores it. At any point in the future, you can then retrieve the information by using certain codes or techniques. Thus, your mind **encodes**, **stores** and **retrieves** information.

Encoding

Encoding is the process by which information is initially taken in. This can be through any of your senses. Some people are more inclined to the **visual**, which means that they can learn better when they see visual aids such as pictures, demonstrations, films, maps, lists, written instructions, etc. While they may pay attention to a lecture in class, visual people may learn better by reading the same lesson from their textbook later or visualizing it in their mind as the teacher is talking. A visual person who is a musician may be able to 'see' the musical notes in his mind while playing from memory.

Some people are more **auditory**, which means that they learn better when they hear something such as spoken instructions, sounds, or noises. Auditory people can understand better when they listen to a lecture rather than when they read or do experiments. They will be able to remember the lyrics of a song after listening to it just once. They can differentiate between the sound of musical instruments in a large orchestra, recognize voices better and pick up foreign languages easily through conversation.

Some people are **kinaesthetic**, which means that they have to touch or feel something to understand it. Kinaesthetic people can learn better by writing down notes, underlining or highlighting in their textbook while studying, doing experiments or even doodling during lectures. Such people would benefit from hands-on experience rather than rote learning.

Most people are a good mix of visual, auditory and kinaesthetic, but may have one dominating trait. Knowing which trait dominates can come in handy when you study since you can modify the method of studying accordingly. The following exercise will give you an idea of what encoding style you prefer.

Exercise 1: Visual Auditory Kinaesthetic Test

Here's a short quiz to check if you are visual, auditory or kinaesthetic. For each of the following statements, circle answers a, b, or c if it describes you best.

1. When I'm anxious about an exam, I
    a) Visualize the absolute worst that can happen.
    b) Talk to myself or others.
    c) Fidget and pace around.

2. When given a project
    a) I can picture what is required.
    b) I tune into what is required.
    c) I get a feeling for what is required.

3. When I am learning something new, I tend to
    a) Write it down first.
    b) Read it out loud.
    c) See if I can draw it.

4. I tend to say
    a) I see what you mean.
    b) I hear you.
    c) I know how you feel.

5. During my free time, I mostly enjoy
    a) Watching TV or videos online.
    b) Listening to music and talking to my friends.
    c) Playing sports or doing some arts and crafts.

6. When I am learning a new skill, I am most comfortable
    a) Watching how the teacher does it.
    b) Getting proper directions from the teacher.
    c) Trying it myself and learning as I go along.

7. When I'm at a concert or watching a music video, I
    a) Notice the band members and other people in the audience.
    b) Listen to the lyrics and the beats.
    c) Dance along to the music.

8. When I concentrate, I mostly
    a) Focus on the words or pictures in front of me.
    b) Discuss the problem and possible solutions with friends.
    c) Fidget a lot, fiddle with pens and pencils, scribble.

9. I find it easier to remember
    a) Faces.
    b) Names.
    c) Activities with friends.

10. When I meet an old friend, I say
    a) It's great to meet you!
    b) It's great to see you again!
    c) I give them a hug or shake their hand.

11. I find it easier to understand a lecture if my teacher
    a) Uses lots of pictures and illustrations.
    b) Speaks clearly with many examples.
    c) Gives us material to work with.

12. I like my house to be
    a) Bright.
    b) Quiet or noisy.
    c) Comfortable.

Now add up your chosen options and write down the total here:
a) _____ b) _____ c) _____

If you chose mostly option (a), you tend to use a visual encoding style. Since you remember best by seeing your study material, you can modify the way you study in the following ways:

- Make your study area visually appealing.
- Make sure you have a designated study area. Since you are a visual person, you may get distracted by the difference in your environment when you sit in a different location.
- Make a lot of notes and lists to help organize your thoughts better. Re-read your notes immediately after class because seeing the written words will reinforce your memory.
- Watch videos and documentaries about the subject that you are studying.
- Use flash cards. Highlight and underline keywords and ideas when you study. Use colour codes for your notes.
- Sit at the front of your class so that you can clearly see the teacher's face and body language.

If you chose mostly option (b), you tend to use an auditory encoding style. Since you remember best by listening, you can modify the way that you study in the following ways:

- Study with a friend or a group. Discuss information. Read lessons out loud or have a friend read it out for you. If you are studying alone, read your notes out loud.
- If possible, record lectures so that you can play it back

and listen to it later.

- Listen to podcasts or audiobooks of your study material.
- When studying, close your eyes to block out visual distractions and focus on hearing the answer, either in your mind or by saying it out loud.
- Sit to the side or at the back of your class so that you can focus more on what your teacher is saying rather than your teacher's face.

If you chose mostly option (c), you tend to use a kinaesthetic encoding style. Since you learn better when you touch and interact with your study material, you can change the way you study in the following ways:

- Walk around your room while you read your study material out loud. Go for a jog or brisk walk while listening to your study material through headphones.
- If you are reading on a computer, mouse-click on the words to give you a physical feedback. If you are reading from your notes or textbook, follow the words with your fingers or with a pen.
- Use flash cards since you can touch them, move them around, shuffle them and interact with them physically.
- Study in short blocks and then indulge in some physical activity such as taking a walk or a quick run up and down some stairs during your break.
- Try to make everything you study more concrete. If you are studying about temples in India, try and visit a few so that you can study the architecture. If you are studying triangles, try and build a triangle with straws and decide on the length of each side, etc.
- Keep trying out different activities and don't force yourself to spend too long on one task. While you study

just as hard as a visual and auditory learner, you may benefit more by switching between subjects rather than spending too much time on one subject.

If you are a blend of two or more styles, it means that you will benefit from any of the techniques applicable to visual, auditory and kinaesthetic encoding, depending on the context or situation.

Storing

Once information is encoded and enters your brain, it needs to be stored so that you can remember it later. The way you store information depends on how interested you are in that particular piece of information, how important it is to you, its function in your life, and for how long you want to store it. For example, you may study your favourite subjects with more enthusiasm than subjects that you find boring. Looking back, you may be able to remember more sections in these subjects than in the ones you found boring.

You may forget your syllabus as soon as your exams get over, or you may forget what you learnt in school as soon as you get home. In this case then, your memory is time bound. Since most of the things that you study are committed to short-term memory, your challenge is to learn how to move that information from short-term memory to long-term memory so that you remember that information for a long time. This is where memory techniques come in. These techniques help you study in such a way that the information gets stored in long-term memory and, therefore, you will be able to remember it at any point in time in the future, not just for exams.

Retrieval

It is not enough just to store information in your brain. You need to be able to remember it or retrieve it for it to be of any use to you. Have you ever studied hard for an exam only to have your mind go blank once you are handed the question paper? This happens because the retrieval cues that you used when you studied were not effective enough.

Do you find that the sight of small children playing brings back memories of your kindergarten days? Or the sound of a train engine rekindles memories of a summer vacation that you took when you were a child? These sights and sounds are called retrieval cues. A retrieval cue helps you locate information stored in your long-term memory. It is something like a search engine on your computer but the cue can be anything from an emotion or a certain word to a particular taste or sound. In the previous section, the retrieval cue that you used was a visualization technique where you pictured George Clooney holding a mouse to remember Moussa Cooney's name. While studying, it is important to have certain cues to remember your syllabus otherwise you may study hard and store all the information in your brain, but your mind may go blank once you start reading the questions in your exam.

Retrieval cues can be a sight, a sound, a taste or even a mood that brings back memories. You will learn retrieval cues more in detail in the following chapters through association, visualization, imagination and location and also by using memory techniques such as acronyms, acrostics, the Link System and Pegging.

Exercise 2: Retrieval Cues

Here is a game that will help you retrieve information better using visual cues. Look at the following pictures for two minutes, then close the book and write down the names of all the pictures you have seen. Once you have written everything down, turn the page for more instructions.

Have you written down all twenty items? If you have, well done! You have great visual memory. If you haven't, here are some retrieval cues.

1. Do you remember any more furniture?
2. Did one piece of furniture stand out from the others?

3. Do you recall any more flowers?
4. Do you remember any more tools?
5. Can you remember using any of these tools before?
6. Can you recollect one picture that is not a furniture, fruit, or tool?

Were you able to remember a few more pictures? Good job! You were able to use the above retrieval cues successfully!

Forgetting

> *'Most people don't forget—they just never take the trouble to remember.'*
> —HARRY LORAYNE

A friend introduces you to a man wearing a bright flowery shirt. Later, you may remember the flowery shirt, but for the life of you, you may not be able to recall the man's name. Why? Perhaps because you did not pay attention to it in the first place because you were distracted by his bright shirt. If the information never entered your mind in the first place, how would it be possible to remember it?

Forgetting happens in any of the three stages of memory—when you fail to encode information, when the information is not stored well or you cannot retrieve the information. In this case, forgetting happened in the initial stage of encoding itself.

Why do you forget? There could be a number of reasons.

- **Interest:** If you are not interested in learning something, you won't bother to encode it. In school, if you find a particular subject boring, you may not be motivated enough to listen to the lecture or jot down notes.
- **Interference:** Something distracted you while you were studying and, while you turned your attention to the

distraction, it pushed out the study material from your mind. This is why it is important to keep away your cell phone while studying. Even if it is on silent mode, the blinking notification light itself is enough to interfere with your concentration.

- **Retrieval Failure:** A friend asks you what movie you watched over the weekend. Although you had looked forward to seeing it, bought the tickets and spent your afternoon watching it, your mind suddenly goes blank and you can't remember the name. The name is at the tip of your tongue, but you still can't remember it. A few hours later, it may suddenly pop into your mind. This is a case of temporary memory loss.

- **Motivated Forgetting:** When you have experienced something traumatic, or you've done badly in an exam, or you were in an embarrassing situation, you may try to purposely forget it or try to block it out from your mind.

- **Constructive Process:** When your memory of something is hazy, you try to fill in the gaps by building on the few things that you do remember. You are therefore trying to construct the memory. Perhaps in your exam, you remember three points out of four. Using those three points, you may try to guess the fourth point as well.

Overcoming Forgetfulness

The first step in overcoming forgetfulness is to **be more observant** of things around you and the things that you do. How often have you forgotten where you left your keys or your spectacles? This happens because you didn't pay attention to where you kept them in the first place. Observation doesn't necessarily mean only things that can be seen. You can also pay attention to the sounds around you or the way certain things make you feel. When you are more aware of the things around you, you will be able to remember them better.

The second step is to **have the motivation** to remember something. Yes, you might think learning chemistry formulae is boring, but you still need to study it. Try to force yourself to be interested enough to study them. I say 'force yourself' because at first, a little effort might be necessary, but in an amazingly short period of time, you will find that there is no effort required to remember any formula that you want if you find ways to motivate yourself to get started.

The third step to overcoming forgetfulness is to **have confidence** in your ability to remember things that you have studied. If you tackle any study material with the belief 'I will remember', more often than not, you will. Think of your memory as a sieve. Each time you say, 'I have an awful memory' or 'I'll never be able to remember this,' you are actually putting another hole in the sieve. On the other hand, if you say, 'I have a wonderful memory' or 'I'll remember this easily,' you're plugging one of the holes.

Exercise 3: Observation Exercise

> **NOT ALL WHO**
> **WANDER ARE**
> **ARE LOST**
> **X**

Read the phrase above. If you have read it, read it again to make sure you know what it says. Now turn your head away from the book and say it out loud. Check again to see if you got it right.

Did you say, 'Not all who wander are lost?' Well, you've got it wrong. If you check the box again, you will see that it actually says, 'Not all who wander are are lost.' There is an extra 'are' in that sentence. If you were right the first time, well done! You have excellent observation skills. Try this out with your friends and see how many get it right the first time.

If you are wondering what the 'X' at the bottom is, it's just placed there as misdirection. It tends to draw the readers' eyes down to it and their minds jump ahead over the phrase itself, because it is such a familiar one.

SUMMARY

- All that you experience and retain through your five senses is called memory.
- Memory is like a muscle—the more you exercise it, the stronger it gets.
- There are three main types of memory—sensory memory, short-term memory and long-term memory.
- Memory works through encoding, storing and retrieval.
- You can be a visual encoder, auditory encoder or kinaesthetic encoder. You can also have a good mix of all three.
- Forgetfulness happens in any of the three stages of memory— either you did not encode the information properly, did not store it well, or did not have proper retrieval cues for it.
- You can overcome forgetfulness by being more observant and motivated and having greater confidence in yourself.

Chapter 2

Building Blocks of Memory

In 2002, Dominic O'Brien entered the Guinness Book of World Records for being able to memorize a random sequence of 2808 playing cards from fifty-four decks of shuffled cards after seeing each card only once. He was correctly able to narrate their order, making only eight errors, four of which he was able to correct when he was told that he was wrong. He is the eight-time winner of the World Memory Championship!

Imagine being able to memorize 2808 cards in sequence. What a great memory he must have. The truth is Dominic O'Brien was often yelled at in school by his teachers for being inattentive, daydreaming in class and not showing much interest in his studies. How did he get from there to being the World Champion of memory? He simply developed his memory skills by practising memory techniques. You can develop your memory too by using these techniques. To use memory techniques effectively, you first need to develop your powers of **visualization**, **association**, **imagination** and memory for **locations** since these are the building blocks of memory.

Visualization

The Greek philosopher Aristotle believed that the human soul never thought without first creating a mental picture. We take in information through our senses, but they are more easily stored and remembered if we convert that information into pictures that we can actually see inside our heads. Have you ever met someone whose name you remembered but not his face? Hardly likely. It usually happens the other way around where you remember the face but not the name. This happens because you've actually *seen* the face while you've *heard* the name and the visual that you have of the face will form a more lasting memory than the sound of the name.

Visualization is nothing but creating pictures or images in your mind. It helps you remember people, places and names easily by associating images, colours and impressions with words. For example, if you want to remember that the capital of Bulgaria is Sofia, you can picture a bull (BULgaria) jumping on a sofa (SOFiA). Make your mental pictures as outrageous, crazy and ridiculous as possible. The image can be animated, brightly coloured or completely out of proportion...whatever works for you. Since all this happens inside your head, you don't have to be afraid of anyone laughing at you or judging you.

Visualizations also help bring your study material to life. For example, if you are learning about the composition of the Lok Sabha, have a mental picture in your head of what a session might look like. In your mind, picture the Lok Sabha to be a palace with the Queen (Speaker of the House, currently Sumitra Mahajan) sitting on her high chair and holding court. All 552 (maximum strength of the Lok Sabha) of her subjects are sitting around her in a semi-circle, facing her. Of the 552 members, 530 are wearing red because they represent their States; twenty are wearing blue because they represent the Union Territories and only two members are wearing bright yellow because they represent the Anglo-Indian community. These two members along with the twenty members of the Union Territories are special because they have been nominated directly by the President of India himself while the other representatives of States have been elected by the people. In your mind, you should be able to see a majority of the people in red, a few people in blue and only two spots of bright yellow. Make sure the picture in your head is as funny, bright and loud as possible. Be as outrageous as you can with your creativity. Can you hear each representative shouting something in their own language? What a cacophony it must be!

Do you think you can remember this picture in your head while writing your exam? I bet you can! Picturing your study material like this is also a good way of moving information from your short-term memory to your long-term memory.

Visualizations do not need to be exact but even picturing any aspect of the object in question is enough for you to be able to recall it. For example, when asked to visualize a horse, you do not need to have an exact picture of a horse in your mind but even an aspect of a horse, such as its glorious silky mane or its polished, shiny horseshoes, is more than enough to fix the mental picture in your mind.

When you are studying long lists of words, you will not have the time to stop and fix a fully accurate mental picture in your mind for every word. What needs to flash in your memory is just a quick image or aspect of the word that you are studying.

Pro Tip: Try to convert your study material into mental images that you can see in your head.

Exercise 1: Visualization Exercise

Try and see a clear image of the following in your mind. Be aware of how they make you feel as well. Try to put in sounds wherever possible.

1. The smell of a new book.
2. The feel of a new currency note.

3. The smell of petrol.
4. Your bed, after a tiring day.
5. The feel of petting a furry puppy.
6. A beautiful sunset.
7. Riding your bike in a light drizzle.
8. The sights, sounds and feel of a beautiful beach.
9. The taste of your favourite ice cream.
10. Hot coffee in winter.

Association

Association simply means connecting two or more things together. Your brain always stores information in the form of connections or associations. Whenever you observe something new, you always connect it with something that you already know. What was subconsciously associated strongly, will be remembered and what was not associated strongly will be forgotten.

It will help you study if you associate any new information with prior information already present in your memory. For example, 'Do Re Me Fa So La Tee Do' (Sa Re Ga Ma Pa Dha Ni Sa) are all associated with the musical notes 'CDEFGABC'. So instead of learning notes as 'C, D, E...' you would learn it as 'Do, Re, Me...', which is easier to remember than individual letters. However, since the words 'Do, Re, Me...' are also words that make little sense, you can associate them with something that you already know. If you know the song from the movie *The Sound of Music*, it goes:

(Do) doe, a deer, a female deer
(Re!) ray, a drop of golden sun
(Mi!) me, a name I call myself
(Fa!) far, a long, long way to run
(So!) sew, a needle pulling thread

(La!) la, a note to follow so
(Ti!) tea, a drink with jam and bread
That will bring us back to do oh oh oh…

Here, not only are the musical notes of 'CDEFGABC' associated with 'Do Re Me Fa So La Tee Do' respectively, but each association of the words (Do Re Me, etc.) is also connected with something that is familiar to you like female deer, sun, needle, thread, etc. This helps you put some meaning to the 'nonsense' words by putting in vivid pictures (a drop of golden sun, needle pulling thread, etc.), thus making it easier to remember.

You may tend to think of an object, not in terms of its dictionary definition but rather by the notions that you associate with it. For example, you may not think of rain as condensed moisture from the atmosphere falling in separate drops, but you may have personal associations for it such as snuggling under the blankets on a rainy day, sitting on the balcony and drinking warm milk while it is pouring outside, bike rides in the rain, slushy puddles, getting splashed, shivering in the cold…the list can go on.

Pro Tip: You learn and remember something new by connecting it with something that you already know, but there is a need to make a strong association between the two. You rarely remember literal definitions of words, but rather a personal or emotional association. How clearly you visualize a picture is more important than how long you can visualize it.

Exercise 2: Association Exercise—Free Association

Read the following words aloud and write down the first thought that you have when you say each word. For example, when you say the word 'swing', you may think of playground, park, kindergarten, etc. There are no wrong answers. Your first association will be the strongest and most significant. Write down as many associations as you like.

Light bulb	Seven	Dawn
Shark	Love	Road trip
Thunder	Ice cream	Library
Project work	Dream	Basketball
Black	Elephant	Shaving cream

Imagination

Imagination is what binds visualizations, associations and locations together. The more absurd the visualization, the stronger is the association and this is achieved by a vivid imagination. Let your imagination run riot. In your head, the laws of physics do not apply. Animals can speak, inanimate objects can juggle or do tricks…anything is possible. The more ridiculous the imagination, the better you will remember what you are studying.

Your dreams are the best gauge of your imagination. The more fantastic your dream, the bigger your imagination. Also, the more often you dream, the better it gets. If you don't remember your dreams, never mind, you can still defy gravity, fight that dragon and rescue that princess, while you're awake! Do not be afraid to daydream. Remember, since all of it will happen inside your head nobody will know about it, let alone laugh at you or judge you.

Where memory is concerned, there are a few fun principles of imagination to follow to make visualizations and associations stronger.

1. **Exaggeration:** The more imaginative and exaggerated your pictorial associations, the better you will remember them. Exaggeration makes your associations unusual and unique.
2. **Out of proportion:** In all your images, try to distort size and shape. Caricatures and cartoons are perfect for this.

3. **Humour:** Be as funny or as rude and obscene as you want. The funnier you are, the better you remember.

4. **Don't just walk, dance!:** It's easy to say 'I went to the bank and deposited the cheque', but it sounds a little mundane. Wouldn't it be more exciting to say 'I crashed into the bank and my cheque went catapulting into the deposit box!' Instead of saying: 'I got bitten by mosquitos', you can say: 'I got massacred by a battalion of mosquitos!' When you use more and more movements and action words in the way you think and express yourself, you will not only remember information better but you will aid your imagination and boost your vocabulary in the process.

5. **'Un' everything:** Unlock, unblock, unleash, unchain, unbar your imagination. Make it as *unusual* as possible.

6. **Sensate:** Use all your senses while visualizing or imagining something. For example, don't just see that strawberry and vanilla ice cream cone in your mind, feel how cool it is in your hands, the slurping sounds you make as you devour it before the cone becomes mushy! Is the smell of strawberries intoxicating? If you use all your senses to imagine something, it leaves a vivid picture in your mind which you will never forget.

7. **Symbols:** Use symbols whenever possible. This not only shortens the time that you need to encode, but gives you a readymade visual. Symbols also help you memorize abstract concepts.

8. **Practice! Practice! Practice!:** And repeat! Yes, you *can* practice daydreaming. The more you practice, the better you will get at it and the quicker you will be able to form images in your mind. Beware of daydreaming during classes though!

9. **Order:** It is easier to remember items that are in order rather than jumbled up or unrelated items. Your brain likes pattern

and logic. If you have jumbled items, take time to put them in some sort of order so that you can understand and associate with them better.

10. **Enjoy:** Perhaps the most important principle to imagination, and indeed, to anything in life, is to enjoy what you are doing. Make studying a game, give yourself rewards for completing something, challenge yourself to memory games and have fun letting your imagination run riot.

Pro Tip: Let your imagination go wild and unfettered when it comes to associating visuals and locations.

Exercise 3: Imagination Exercise

By some strange good fortune, you now own a world-famous sculpture which is heavy and is about the size of your palm. Write down as many possible uses for it that you can think of. Time yourself, take only two minutes. Award yourself one point for common answers and two points for imaginative answers. Now check your scores:

20 or more: Highly creative	7–10: Good
16–19: Excellent	3–6: Average
11–15: Very Good	0–2: Poor

Examples for common answers: Put it in the showcase/Insure it/ Put it in a safe or a locker.

Examples for imaginative answers: Use it as a door stop/Use it to balance scales/Use it as a garden ornament.

Location

Locations make up the map of memory, providing a natural and efficient way of storing and retrieving memories. This is because the world is three-dimensional and objects can be located—physically or mentally—by where they are placed or located. Where memory is concerned, the trick is to visualize a location that is familiar to you such as your house, school or the route that you take to school. Identify landmarks along these routes and then picture what you want to memorize on each landmark.

For example, if your location is your house, you can picture your front door as the first landmark, the shoe rack as your second landmark, your sofa in the living room as the third, and so on. If you were given a list of items to buy at the supermarket such as milk, eggs, bread, curd, cornflakes, etc. you can picture each of these at each landmark. For example, you can picture a carton of milk at your front door (first landmark), the eggs on top of your shoe rack (second landmark) and bread on your sofa (third landmark), and so on. When you need to remember the list, all you need to do is mentally walk through your house starting at your front door, and you will be able to see each item at each location! This is how you can visualize and associate objects with familiar locations in order to remember better.

Just as it is possible to find a connection between any two sets of information, it is possible for your brain to find an association between any word, object, notion, or thought and a location. Let's take the word 'crayon', for instance. Close your eyes and let your mind wander freely, thinking about this word. Your mind may take you to several places such as your pre-school where you did a lot of colouring, or your grandparents' house where they always kept a box of crayons for you, or a friend's birthday party where you played a party game and won some crayons, or a restaurant where you were given two crayons along with the kids' menu, etc. Location, then, is an indispensable building block of memory training because it lends itself well to association.

Pro Tip: Visualizing and associating something new or something to be learnt with familiar location routes will help strengthen the image in your mind.

Exercise 4: Location Exercise

Look at the following words and write down the images that pop in your mind while reading them. Once these images pop up, observe the location or places where they occur.

Cloudy	Pizza	Picnic
Blue	Grandfather	Happy
Dog	Snow	Swim
Crash	Fun	Prize
Kiss	Movie	Cricket

SUMMARY

- The building blocks of memory are visualization, association, imagination and location.
- With all the above building blocks, make sure you see a clear image in your mind.
- Make the associations in your mind as absurd, ridiculous and rude as possible—you will remember it better.
- Make sure you see the image in connection with a location— don't just imagine it hanging in mid-air.
- Use familiar locations and images. The key is to learn something new by associating it with something that you are already familiar with.

Chapter 3

Memory Techniques

PART ONE: FUN MEMORY TECHNIQUES

Acronyms

Using acronyms is the easiest method for remembering information, where you take the first letter of each word to be remembered and this, in turn, may (or may not) form another word. Here, the first letter of each word serves as a clue to an item that you need to recall. This is useful when you want to remember words in a specific order, but it is more helpful in just shortening long words to their abbreviations. For example, United Nations Organization is simply shortened to UNO but most of the time, you may just say 'UN'.

Some common acronyms are:

BBC — British Broadcasting Corporation
NATO — The North Atlantic Treaty Organization
SCUBA — Self-Contained Underwater Breathing Apparatus
NBA — National Basketball Association
LASER — Light Amplification by Stimulated Emission of Radiation
NASA — National Aeronautics and Space Administration
SAARC — The South Asian Association for Regional Cooperation
ASEAN — The Association of Southeast Asian Nations

OPEC   —   The Organization of the Petroleum Exporting Countries

When you text or chat online, you may use a lot of acronyms such as:

LOL	—	Laughing Out Loud
OMG	—	Oh My God
BRB	—	Be Right Back
TTYL	—	Talk To You Later
PS	—	Postscript

You may use many acronyms on a day-to-day basis as well. Some of these are:

ASAP	—	As Soon As Possible
ADR	—	Address
PTO	—	Please Turn Over
AWOL	—	Absent Without Official Leave
BF/GF	—	Boyfriend/Girlfriend

How can you apply acronyms while studying? If there is a short enough list of words, you can simply take the first letter of each word and combine them. When you see the initial letters, you should be reminded of the whole word. For example, if you wanted to learn the names of oceans from the largest to the smallest, you can use the acronym '**PAISA**' to represent **P**acific Ocean, **A**tlantic Ocean, **I**ndian Ocean, **S**outhern Ocean and **A**rctic Ocean.

Let's look at a few more examples that may be useful to you while studying.

History and Civics

1. Official languages of the UN: FACERS—**F**rench, **A**rabic, **C**hinese, **E**nglish, **R**ussian, **S**panish.

2. Members of OPEC: QUAKE IS LEAVING—Qatar, UAE, Algeria, Kuwait, Ecuador, Iran, Saudi Arabia, Libya, Equatorial Guinea, Angola, Venezuela, Iraq, Nigeria, Gabon.

3. The full list of Mughal Emperors who ruled in India: BHAJ SABJi FaRS MAA SSAAB

B–Babur	S–Shah Jahan	Fa–Farrukhsiyar
H–Humayun	A–Alamgir	R–Rafi ud-Darajat
A–Akbar	B–Bahadur	S–Shah Jahan II
J–Jahangir	Ji–Jahandar Shah	

M–Muhhamad Shah	S–Shah Jahan III
A–Ahmad Shah	S–Shah Alam III
A–Alamgir II	A–Akbar Shah II
	B–Bahadur Shah II

4. Who fought the first Anglo–Mysore war?
    Hyder Ali vs MEN—Maratha, English, Nizams.

5. Invaders of India in sequence:
    PDEF—Portugal, Dutch, English, French.

6. Where was the Harappa civilization located?
    GPRS—Gujarat, Punjab, Rajasthan, Sind.

7. States with Bicameral System:
    JUMBAKT—Jammu & Kashmir, Uttar Pradesh, Maharashtra, Bihar, Andhra Pradesh, Karnataka, Telangana.

8. Sessions of Lok Sabha:
    BMW
    B—Budget (February to May)
    M—Monsoon (June to September)
    W—Winter (November to December)

Geography

1. Colours of the rainbow: VIBGYOR—**V**iolet, **I**ndigo, **B**lue, **G**reen, **Y**ellow, **O**range, **R**ed.
   ROY G BIV—**R**ed, **O**range, **Y**ellow, **G**reen, **B**lue, **I**ndigo, **V**iolet.

2. Countries collectively called the Horn of Africa: SEED—**S**omalia, **E**thiopia, **E**ritrea, **D**jibouti.

3. Length of boundaries that India shares with surrounding countries in decreasing order: BaChPaN MBA—**BA**ngladesh, **CH**ina, **PA**kistan, **N**epal, **M**yanmar, **B**hutan, **A**fghanistan.

4. Seven mountain ranges of India: V SHAPES—**V**indhyas, **S**atpuras, **H**imalayas, **A**ravalis, **P**atkai, **E**astern Ghats, **S**ahyadris.

5. ASEAN Countries: BLIMPS C MTV—**B**runei, **L**aos, **I**ndonesia, **M**alaysia, **P**hilippines, **S**ingapore, **C**ambodia, **M**yanmar, **T**hailand, **V**ietnam.

6. G7 Economies: JUICE GF

J—**J**apan	G—**G**ermany
U—**U**SA	F—**F**rance
I—**I**taly	(European Union is also part of this group, represented by above mentioned European Countries)
C—**C**anada	
E—**E**ngland (UK)	

7. SAARC Countries: MBBS PAIN

M—Maldives	P—Pakistan
B—Bangladesh	A—Afghanistan
B—Bhutan	I—India
S—Sri Lanka	N—Nepal

8. Core Industries of India: CCC FRENS

C—Coal	F—Fertilizers
C—Crude Oil	R—Refinery Products
C—Cement	E—Electricity
	N—Natural Gas
	S—Steel

Mathematics

1. The order of operations in Maths (USA): PEMDAS—**P**arenthesis, **E**xponents, **M**ultiplication, **D**ivision, **A**ddition, **S**ubtraction.

2. The order of operations in Maths (UK, India and Australia): BODMAS—**B**rackets, **O**rder (**O**f), **D**ivision, **M**ultiplication, **A**ddition, **S**ubtraction.

3. Factoring Binomials: FOIL—**F**irst, **O**uter, **I**nner, **L**ast.

4. How to solve a word problem: SOLVE—**S**tudy the problem, **O**rganize the facts, **L**ine up the plan, **V**erify the plan with computation, **E**xamine the answer.

5. Method for dividing fractions: SMURF—**S**ame, **M**ultiply, **U**pside-down, **R**ename **F**raction.

6. Multiplying two-digit numbers by two-digit numbers: MOMA—**M**ultiply, **A**dd the **0**, **M**ultiply, **A**dd.

Biology

1. The phases of mitosis: IPMAT—**I**nterphase, **P**rophase, **M**etaphase, **A**naphase, **T**elophase.

2. ABC of an environment: ABC—**A**biotic (non-living), **B**iotic (living), **C**ultural (man-made).

3. Eight aspects of living organisms: GRRIM END—**G**rowth, **R**espiration, **R**eproduction, **I**rritability, **M**ovement, **E**xcretion, **N**utrition, **D**eath.

English

1. The eight parts of speech in English: PAV PANIC— **P**ronouns, **A**djectives, **V**erbs, **P**repositions, **A**dverbs, **N**ouns, **I**nterjections, **C**onjunctions.

2. The seven coordinating conjunctions in English: FANBOYS— **F**or, **A**nd, **N**or, **B**ut, **O**r, **Y**et, **S**o.

Scriptures

1. The seven deadly sins: PALE GAS—**P**ride, **A**varice, **L**ust, **E**nvy, **G**luttony, **A**nger, **S**loth.

2. Code of conduct of Buddha: V CLIP
    V—no **V**iolence
    C—no **C**orruption
    L—no **L**ies
    I—no **I**ntoxicants
    P—no coveting **P**roperty of others

3. Three principles of Jainism, also called Triratnas: KFC
    K—right **K**nowledge
    F—right **F**aith
    C—right **C**onduct

Music

1. The space notes on the treble clef stave: FACE—**F**, **A**, **C**, **E**.

There are a few disadvantages to this system. The first is that if there is more than one word that begins with the same letter, you might get confused about the order of the words. To remedy this, you can take the first two letters of the second word to form an acronym. The second disadvantage is that this method is useful for rote memory, but does not help with comprehension of information. The third disadvantage is that acronyms don't always work for every type of information. Some combination of initials of words may not always lead to another memorable word or short-form. The fourth disadvantage is that there is a danger of forgetting the acronym itself, which will lead to a failure to retrieve the necessary information. This is why, as with any other memory technique, care should be taken to encode and learn the information at the beginning.

Keep in mind that you need to learn the information in the first place. Acronyms are only memory aids that help you retrieve the information already learnt. For example, you may be able to remember the acronym V CLIP, but unless you know what it stands for, remembering the acronym alone is useless.

Acrostics

Acrostics are similar to acronyms, but you take the first letter of each word and form sentences with them. It is a 'poem or any other form of writing in which the first letter, syllable, or word of each line, paragraph, or other recurring feature in the text spells out a word or a message.' For example, the names of the planets in our solar system can be remembered in order by using the acrostic **My Very Elegant Mother Just Served Us Noodles**. When you take the first letter of each word, you get **Mercury, Venus, Earth, Mars, Jupiter, Saturn, Uranus** and **Neptune**. Just by remembering the sentence or phrase, you will get the first letters of all the words that you need to remember. This method is handy in remembering passwords, formulae and long lists of words that need to be memorized in order. This method is less limiting than acronyms. If your words don't form easy to remember acronyms, you can just make up ridiculous sentences to remember them.

Biology

1. In Taxonomy, you can remember the order of rankings by remembering this acrostic:
   Keep Pots Clean Otherwise Families Get Sick
   Kingdom, Phylum, Class, Order, Family, Genus, Species

2. Phases of mitosis:
   I Picked Many Apples Today/I Propose Men Are Toads
   Interphase, Prophase, Metaphase, Anaphase, Telophase

3. The levels of organization from smallest to biggest in Ecology:
   Idiot, Please Carry Everyone's Biology Books
   Individual, Population, Community, Ecosystem, Biome, Biosphere

4. The eight facial bones:
   Varun Can Make My Pet Zebra Laugh
   Vomer, Conchae, Nasal, Maxilla, Mandible, Palatine, Zygomatic, Lacrimal

5. The eight wrist bones:
   She Looks Too Pretty, Try To Catch Her
   Scaphoid, Lunate, Triquetrum, Pisiform, Trapezium, Trapezoid, Capitate, Hamate

Mathematics

1. Trigonometric Ratios:

   Sin = Perpendicular/Hypotenuse Some People Have

   Cos = Base/Hypotenuse Curly Black Hair

   Tan = Perpendicular/Base Turning Permanently Brown

2. Which trigonometry functions are positive in each of the four quadrants of the Cartesian Coordinate plane?
   All Seniors Take Calculus
   Quad I: All functions are positive.
   Quad II: Only **S**ine is positive.
   Quad III: Only **T**angent is positive.
   Quad IV: Only **C**osine is positive.

3. Metric System:
   King Henry Died By Drinking Chocolate Milk
   Kilo, Hecto, Deca, Base, Deci, Centi, Milli

4. Dividing fractions:
   Can Fred Multiply?
   - Change the division to multiplication.
   - Flip the second fraction.
   - Multiply.

5. Circumference of a circle:
   Cherry Pies, Delicious!
   $C = pi \times d$ where C is the circumference and d is the diameter.

6. Area of a circle:
   Apple Pies aRe Square
   $A = pi \times r^2$ where A is area and r is radius

7. Roman numerals:
   I Value Xylophones Like Cows Dig Milk
   $I = 1, V = 5, X = 10, L = 50, C = 100, D = 500, M = 1000$

Chemistry

1. First 20 elements in the periodic table:
   Happy Henry Lives Beside Boron Cottage, Near Our Friend Nelly Nancy MgAllen. Silly Patrick Stays Close. Arthur

Kisses **Carrie**.

H—Hydrogen, **He**—Helium, **Li**—Lithium, **Be**—Beryllium, **B**—Boron, **C**—Carbon, **N**—Nitrogen, **O**—Oxygen, **F**—Fluorine, **Ne**—Neon, **Na**—Sodium, **Mg**—Magnesium, **Al**—Aluminium, **Si**—Silicon, **P**—Phosphorus, **S**—Sulphur, **Cl**—Chlorine, **Ar**—Argon, **K**—Potassium, **Ca**—Calcium.

2. Electrochemical Cell: Oxidation vs Reduction
   AN OIL RIG CAT
   At the **AN**ode, **O**xidation **I**nvolves **L**oss of electrons. **R**eduction **I**nvolves **G**aining electrons at the **CAT**hode.

3. Diatomic molecules:
   I Have **N**o **B**right **O**r **C**lever **F**riends.
   Iodine, **H**ydrogen, **N**itrogen, **B**romine, **O**xygen, **C**hlorine, **F**luorine.

4. Carboxylic Acids (first six):
   Frogs **A**re **P**olite, **B**eing **V**ery **C**ourteous.
   Formic, **A**cetic, **P**ropionic, **B**utyric, **V**aleric, **C**aproic.

5. Dicarboxylic Acids (first nine):
   Oh **M**y! **S**uch **G**reat **A**pple **P**ie! **S**weet **A**s **S**ugar!
   Oxalic, **M**alonic, **S**uccinic, **G**lutaric, **A**dipic, **P**imelic, **S**uberic, **A**zelaic, **S**ebacic.

Physics

1. Electromagnetic Spectrum: In order of decreasing wavelength of electromagnetic waves.
   Ronald **M**cDonald **I**nvented **V**ery **U**nusual and **E**xcellent **G**um.
   Radio waves, **M**icrowaves, **I**nfrared, **V**isible light, **U**ltraviolet, **X**-Rays, **G**amma Rays.

2. Electromagnetic Spectrum: In order of increasing wavelength of electromagnetic waves.
   Good **X**ylophones **U**se **V**ery **I**nteresting **M**usical **R**hythms.
   Gamma Rays, **X**-rays, **U**ltraviolet, **V**isible light, **I**nfrared, **M**icrowaves, **R**adio Waves.

3. Relationship between focal length and object, and the object and image distance from a lens or mirror:
   If I do I die
   $1/f = 1/do\text{-}1/di$

4. Colour codes used in electronics, in numerical order:
   Billy **B**rown **R**ealized **O**nly **Y**esterday, **G**ood **B**oys **V**alue **G**ood **W**ork.
   Black (0), **B**rown (1), **R**ed (2), **O**range (3), **Y**ellow (4), **G**reen (5), **B**lue (6), **V**iolet (7), **G**rey (8), **W**hite (9).

Geography

1. Rivers in North-West India:
   I **J**ust **C**hecked **B**eautiful **R**iver **S**urveys.
   Indus, **J**helum, **C**henab, **B**eas, **R**avi, **S**atluj.

2. Levels of atmosphere:
   Typical, **S**uper **M**ario's **T**ime **E**xpired.
   Troposphere, **S**tratosphere, **M**esosphere, **T**hermosphere, **E**xosphere.

3. Water Cycle:
   Every **C**ook **P**eels **R**ed **O**nions.
   Evaporation, **C**ondensation, **P**recipitation, **R**unoff, **O**cean.

Music

1. The space notes on the bass clef stave:
   All **C**ows **E**at **G**rass.
   A, C, E, G.

2. The line notes on the bass clef stave:
   Grizly **B**ears **D**on't **F**ly **A**eroplanes.
   G, B, D, F, A.

3. The line notes on the treble clef stave:
   Every **G**ood **B**oy **D**eserves **F**ruit.
   E, G, B, D, F.

French

1. Days of the week in French:
   Large **M**ean **M**onkeys **J**umped **V**ery **S**lowly **D**own.
   Lundi, **M**ardi, **M**ercredi, **J**eudi, **V**endredi, **S**amedi, **D**imanche.

While studying, try and make your own acrostics—you will remember them better. As with acronyms, acrostics are simply a memory aid but do not help with understanding or comprehension of the information. The disadvantage is that you may forget the phrase or sentence or may substitute words with similar words and therefore, get the initials wrong. Knowing the acrostic is not enough—you need to learn the information first. For example, just remembering 'Large mean monkeys jumped very slowly down' may only lead you to the initials of LMMJVSD, but unless you know what they stand for using acrostics would be pointless.

Rhymes and Music

Just as the 'ABC' song, 'Twinkle Twinkle Little Star' and 'Baa Baa Black Sheep' have a familiar tune. You can put your study material into a familiar song so that you can remember it just by singing it. This works with any kind of information, including formulae and definitions.

For example, facts about an isosceles triangle can be learnt by singing the following to the tune of 'Oh Christmas Tree'.

Oh, isosceles, oh, isosceles,
Two angles have equal degrees.
Oh, isosceles, oh, isosceles
You look just like a Christmas tree.

You can make up a rhyme about anything that you are studying, which makes your study material easier to remember. Some examples are given below.

1. *In the year 1947, India reached Independence heaven!*

2. *In 1492, Columbus sailed the ocean blue!*

3. Converting a pint to a pound: *A pint is a pound the whole world around!*

4. Area and circumference of a circle:
    Tweedle-dum and Tweedle-dee,
    Around the circle is pi times d,
    But if the area is declared,
    Think of the formula pi 'r' squared.
   'Around the circle' is the circumference.
   Circumference = pi × d (diameter).
   Area = pi x r (radius) squared.

5. In chemistry, always remember to add acid to water and **not** the other way around!

    Always do things as you oughta
    Add the acid to the water.
    If you think your life's too placid,
    Add the water to the acid.

6. When multiplying with negative numbers, is the answer positive or negative? Here's a way to remember. This is not a rhyme, but it makes it easier to understand the outcome

of multiplying with negative numbers. (In this technique, 'good' is positive and 'bad' is negative.)

A good thing happening to a good person is good. (Positive x positive = positive.)
A good thing happening to a bad person is bad. (Positive x negative = negative.)
A bad thing happening to a good person is bad. (Negative x positive = negative.)
A bad thing happening to a bad person is good. (Negative x negative = positive.)

Number Phrase Technique

This technique helps you remember long numbers just by using the same number of letters in words as the number. For example, 'my' has two letters, so denotes the number 2. 'Terrible' has eight letters and so denotes the number 8.

Do you want to learn the value of pi up to the fifteenth digit? Here it is! All you need to do is remember this phrase and count the number of letters in each word and you have your answer!

Value of pi: 3.14159265358979

How I want a drink, alcoholic of course, after the heavy lectures involving quantum mechanics.

| 3 | 1 | 4 | 1 | 5 | 9 | 2 | 6 | 5 | 3 | 5 | 8 | 9 | 7 | 9 |

or

May I have a large container of coffee?

| 3 | 1 | 4 | 1 | 5 | 9 | 2 | 6 |

or

How I wish I could calculate pi

| 3 | 1 | 4 | 1 | 5 | 9 | 2 |

a) Value of 'e' (exponential function) up to the eighth digit: 2.7182818

To express 'e', remember to memorize a sentence

2   7   1   8   2   8   1   8

or

By omnibus I travelled to Brooklyn

2   7   1   9   2   8

b) Speed of light in metres per second: 2.99792458

We guarantee certainly, clearly referring to this light mnemonic

2   9   9   7   9   2 4   5   8

Exercise 1: Number Phrase

Try to make up your own phrases for the numbers listed below. The first example is worked out for you.

1. Your ATM PIN is 8464. Now look for eight letter words, four letter words, six letter words and four letter words.

8   4   6   4

Martians were coming home

Now, every time you go to the ATM, all you need to do is count the letters per word in this phrase 'Martians were coming home' and you will remember your PIN number.

2. Try this with your friend's house number.

5   2   5   3

_____ _____ _____ _____

3. Your lock combination.

        4   8   5   4

    ____ ____ ____ ____

4. Your student ID number.

        3   3   7   3   5

    ____ ____ ____ ____ ____

5. The Sepoy Movement started in India in the year 1857. How would you remember this date?

    ____ ____ ____ ____ ____

6. The atomic number of Potassium (K) is 19.

    ____ ____

7. Your bike's licence plate number (or your friend's).

    ____ ____ ____ ____

8. Your own ATM PIN number.

    ____ ____ ____ ____

9. The year when your parents got married.

    ____ ____ ____ ____

10. The year that you were born.

    ____ ____ ____ ____

With this technique, be careful to remember the phrase or sentence word for word. If you substitute a word or add or subtract a word, the corresponding number will be wrong. For example, instead of 'large container,' if you say 'big container', you will get the value of pi wrong because you will be writing down a 3 (b-i-g) instead of a 5 (l-a-r-g-e).

Mental Snapshot Technique

'While writing an exam, all I had to do was close my eyes and visualize the answer. Sometimes, I could see the textbook page clearly in my mind and all I had to do was copy the answer from the picture in my head.'

This technique helps you take a mental photograph or a snapshot of your surroundings and saves the image in your mind. By engaging your full concentration in the present moment, this technique encourages the formation of clearer, stronger memories of important scenes. This method uses three basic and simple memory skills: looking, snapping and then connecting.

How do you 'snap' a picture? This is nothing but making sure that the picture is 'burnt' into your mind. You can do this by blinking your eyes and imagining that they are the shutter of a camera. This is a kinaesthetic way of doing it. You can add audio to it by hearing a 'click' of a camera shutter while you do this.

If you are on holiday and you would like to remember the scenery, you first look closely and pay attention to the scene, create a mental snapshot of that scene and then connect it with the town or city that you are in. For example, you're on a beach in Goa, watching an amazing sunset. First, pay attention to the details around you. There may be children playing in the sand nearby, the sky may be multi-coloured, the ocean may be reflecting the sunlight and changing colour accordingly. Fix your gaze on the image that you would like to 'burn' into your memory and then capture it in your mind. This means that when you close your eyes, you should be able to see this image clearly in your mind. Now connect this image to the place. For example, Goa, 2018. In the future, whenever you think of this vacation or of a sunset or Goa, you will always have this image in your mind.

If you are studying for your algebra exam and you would like to remember a quadratic equation, first look at it. Observe the equation and all its components. Here, x is the unknown while a, b and c are constants.

$$x = \frac{-b \pm \sqrt{b^2 - 4ac}}{2a}$$

Once you have observed the equation, the next step is to snap your picture. Make sure that the image of the equation is 'burnt' into your mind so that you can still see it when you close your eyes.

The third step is to make connections so that if someone asks you what the quadratic equation is, you should be able to immediately recall this image.

The Mental Snapshot Technique is generally used to remember names and faces. But you can also use it to picture formulae and diagrams from your textbooks.

Exercise 2: Mental Snapshot of a Biology Diagram

Look at any diagram in your biology textbook. Observe all the details. Close your eyes and see if you can see the image clearly in your mind. If you cannot, open your eyes and observe the details you might have missed. Repeat this process till you are sure that you can picture all the details in your mind. Now close the book and see if you can draw it without looking.

SUMMARY

Acronyms

- Take the first letters of each word to be remembered and group them together.
- Acronyms can be used to remember lists that are not too long.

Acrostics

- Take the first letter of each word to be remembered and make another word to form a sentence or phrase.
- Acrostics can be used to remember long numbers and long pieces of information in sequence.

Rhymes and Music

- Putting your study material into a rhyme or a tune can help you remember it better.

Number Phrase Technique

- The number of letters per word needs to correspond to the number being remembered.
- The words themselves do not matter, only the number of letters that they have matters.
- This technique can be used to remember very long numbers.

Mental Snapshot Method

- Three steps—Look, Snap and Connect.
- When you 'snap' you should be able to see the image clearly in your mind when you close your eyes.
- You can use this method to remember names and faces, holidays, scenery, diagrams, formulae, etc.

Chapter 4

Memory Techniques

PART TWO: LINKING

Learning Through Linking

The Link System of memory is one of the easiest techniques to master. It makes use of all the building blocks of memory but relies heavily on association and visualization. This system can be used to memorize anything in sequence such as speeches, lists, daily schedules, errands, long numbers, formulae, recipes, history timelines, etc. Simply put, it functions by associating items with each other by using your imagination in the most ridiculous, funny, or bizarre way. There are two link methods—the Pure Link Method and the Story Link Method.

Pure Link Method

Do you think you can remember a list of twenty unrelated words in the correct order? Of course, you can! Let's see how to go about it. Here are the words:

telephone, shadow, paper, fish, violin, bed, rose, book,
chicken, sun, cheese, umbrella, window, mall,
ice cream, carpet, computer, mangoes, shampoo, cat

Okay, now let's see how to link these words so that they can be remembered in order. Since your brain tends to remember and associate things in pairs, you will need to work with two words at a time. Here, two words form one link. First take words 1 and 2, then 2 and 3, then 3 and 4, and so on.

The first pair to remember is telephone and shadow. Now, the most practical picture that would come to mind may be a shadow holding a telephone to its ear, but your aim is to make the images in your mind as bright, loud and absurd as possible so that you can remember the associations easily. Can you picture a pink shadow juggling five telephones in its hands? Or imagine rubbing a telephone and a shadow pops out of it like a genie from a lamp! See that image clearly in your mind.

Now move on to words 2 and 3—shadow and paper. When you move on to the next set of words, the previous word is ignored for the time being. So putting the word telephone aside, focus on shadow and paper. Imagine a shadow made of paper, being blown about by the wind while on his evening walk. Fix that image in your mind.

Words 3 and 4—paper and fish. Keep the word shadow aside for now and focus on paper and fish. Can you picture a fish somersaulting over a sea of paper? Every time the fish 'splashes' down, a sheaf of papers flies all over the place like a fountain.

Fish and violin—you're playing a violin at a big concert but instead of a bowstring, you are using a fish!

Violin and bed—a bed made of violins that plays music to you as you fall asleep. You don't even need an alarm clock in the morning since you have your violin bed to wake you up!

Bed and rose—you wake up in bed to find hundreds of rose petals cascading around you gently. All of a sudden, that gentle shower of petals becomes heavy, spikey roses, forcing you to take cover under your bed!

Rose and book—a book's pages made of rose petals and bookmarked with paper.

Book and chicken—you enter class, and, sitting in your

teacher's chair, is a gigantic chicken wearing reading glasses, squinting at a book. It looks at you over its glasses. 'Surprise!' it squawks in a dry voice.

Chicken and sun—as the sun rises, you open your windows to let the sunshine in, but instead a brood of chickens bursts in and start watching TV.

Can you work out the rest of the words?

Sun and cheese_____

Cheese and umbrella_____

Umbrella and window_____

Window and mall_____

Mall and ice cream _____

Ice cream and carpet_____

Carpet and computer_____

Computer and mangoes_____

Mangoes and shampoo_____

Shampoo and cat_____

Now close your eyes and see the associations clearly in your mind starting from telephone and ending with cat. Were you able to remember all twenty words? Good job! Shall we make it a bit tougher? Try to recall all twenty words backwards from cat to telephone moving backwards in the links. Write them down here:

_____	_____	_____	_____
_____	_____	_____	_____
_____	_____	_____	_____
_____	_____	_____	_____
_____	_____	_____	

Story Link Method

Another method for linking unrelated words is to make up a story using all the words in the same sequence. We'll use the same words as above.

Once upon a time, in the land of **telephone**, there lived a **shadow** who liked to juggle. He could juggle anything from **papers** to **fish** to **violins**! He was so good at juggling that he could do it even lying down on his **bed** or upside down! Other shadows came from all over the world to watch his performances. They would often throw **roses** on stage to show their appreciation or **books** or **chickens** at him if they did not like his act. Since shadows often disappear when the **sun** is out, he carried a **cheese umbrella** and avoided all **windows**. At the **mall,** the shadow gulped down an **ice cream** which made him feel woozy and he fainted right there on the **carpet**! They used the mall **computer** to order **mango**-flavoured **shampoo** to revive him. He then went home to juggle his shadow **cat**!

Pro Tips:

- Make the images in your mind as bright, loud and absurd as possible.
- As you make up the story, *visualize* it happening. This is what drills it into your long-term memory. If you can see it in your mind's eye like a movie, you'll automatically remember

it afterwards.

- Don't be practical. Be as fanciful as you like. Your mind remembers flights of fancy better than practicalities.
- When moving from the first set of linked words, set the first word aside while moving on to the next pair. For example, after pairing 1 and 2, set 1 aside while you move on to 2 and 3. Remember that you are always associating the previous object to the present object.
- Use your own visuals. Usually, the first thought that pops into your head is the best one.
- Take only about a split second per association. You may take longer at first but as you practice associations, you will be able to conjure up visual images in an instant! Although the above explanations are long, the actual exercise will take you only two or three minutes.
- Do not try to visualize the words themselves, but focus on the pictures that they bring to your mind.
- To remember the first word of the list, link it to something else that you are familiar with. Make it a personal association—something that is connected to you. For example, since telephone is the first word here, picture a giant telephone that hops around and buzzes your name every time it rings. Now that you have remembered the first word, start linking it to the next.
- In case you forget a word, try and remember the next word and then work your way backwards.

Broken Links

If you forget a word in the link, it could be that the association that you made between words was not strong enough or the image in your mind was too dull or not memorable enough to begin with. If this happens, try and remember another word in the sequence and work your way backwards.

Perhaps your visualization of a word was a bit too abstract. Since you are given barely one second per word, you may see a hazy picture floating mid-air. If you were to give this picture some context, you will add a backdrop to it, which can serve as a visual cue later when you recall the word. For example, if you had pictured a land covered with telephones while reading the first sentence of the story above, you would have given the shadow a good context for his juggling.

While the pure link method is more or less reliable, the story link method is not so reliable as you may deviate from the original plot of the story and forget the sequence or even the words that you need to remember! This is why it is important to **see** the associations clearly in your mind. If you are using the story link method, try to see the story like a movie in your head.

Since you may not remember all the words in sequence in the story link method, use it for lists that do not require an order or a sequence, such as a shopping list or your chores for the day. Use the pure link method to remember the sequence of events in history or a speech or a telephone number.

Exercise 1: Linking Items in a Shopping List

You need to go to the supermarket to do your grocery shopping. Using either the Pure Link Method or the Story Link Method, try to remember your shopping list.

Tip: Picture where each item is inside the supermarket and add their locations to your associations as context.

chicken, milk, corn, potatoes, eggs, bread, brinjal, cupcakes, flour, cooking chocolate, fresh cream, butter, cheese, cornflakes, pancake mix, carrots, peas, mushrooms, coconuts

SUMMARY

- The Link System can be used to memorize anything in sequence such as speeches, lists, daily schedules, errands, long numbers, formulae, recipes, history timelines, etc.
- It works by associating one word interacting with the next word.
- It helps you remember words and lists in their correct order.

Pure Link System

- This system works by associating the first word interacting with the second word, the second word interacting with the third word, the third word interacting with the fourth word and so on.

Story Link System

- This system works by making up a story using all the words to be remembered.

Chapter 5

Memory Techniques

PART THREE: PEGGING

While the Linking method is easy and effective, it is possible to break the chain of associations by forgetting just one item. In the Link System, random words are associated with random images. Through the Pegging method, there is an established list of images or words that will never change. Using these pre-determined images or words as a base, you can then link new information to them by visualizing, imagining and associating the new images with the images or words that you already have in your mind. Pegging not only allows you to remember items in their correct order, but also helps you remember the item's exact position on the list.

Imagine your cupboard full of hangers and clothes hanging on each of them. While the hangers never change, the clothes you hang on them will keep changing. This is the same principle that is used in Pegging. While your memory pegs never change, what you associate with them will keep changing. From now on, you will be able to 'hang' anything you wish to remember involving numbers or letters in any way, on these pegs!

Memory pegs are things that you know well, in a set order. There are two basic pegs—pegs for numbers and pegs for letters. To memorize a list, you associate the first item to the first peg, the second item to the second peg and so on. In case you forget an item, you can leave that peg empty and move on. You will be able to remember the next peg since remembering it does not depend on remembering the previous peg like the Link System does.

On a daily basis, you need to be able to remember your credit card number, Aadhaar card number, telephone numbers, ATM PINs, passwords, addresses, student identification number, etc. Since numbers are abstract concepts, they have very little meaning. The Number Shape System, the Number Rhyme System and the Major System of Number Pegging will help you ascribe some meaning to these numbers by associating them with specific words or pictures, which you can then visualize better by using your imagination. The Alphabet Peg System can help you memorize long lists of words, schedules, poems, speeches, etc. in their correct order.

As with everything related to studying, the key is to keep revising the lists in the Number Peg System and the Alphabet Peg System until the numbers and letters along with their respective associated images are second nature to you. Here's how you can do this:

1. Read through the numbers and alphabets with their associated peg words.
2. Close your eyes and run through the numbers from 0 to 10 and alphabets from A to Z, seeing a colourful and bright picture of each key rhyming word, shape or image clearly in your mind.
3. Run through the list from 0 to 10 and from A to Z in the usual order.
4. Now run through the list in reverse order.
5. Next, think of the numbers and letters in random order.
6. Finally, conjure up the images in your mind and link them to their associated number or letter.

7. Repeat steps 1 through 6 until you are thorough with the numbers and letters and their pegs. You need to get to the point where your mind instantly produces the images when you think of the numbers or the letters.

THE NUMBER PEG SYSTEM

The Number Peg System consists of three systems namely—the Number Shape System, the Number Rhyme System and the Major System. These systems are important and are used to memorize history dates, anniversaries and long numbers such as telephone numbers, Aadhaar card numbers, passport numbers, credit card numbers, etc.

The Number Shape System

This system is easy and uses only numbers from 0 to 10. This memory technique works by associating specific numbers to an image that resembles that particular number. Each image should essentially be the same shape or a similar shape to its corresponding number. For example, the open sails of a sailboat resemble the number 4 while the curved trunk of an elephant resembles the number 6. Initially, you will need to take time to memorize the image that each number denotes but with a little practice, you will be able to convert numbers to their corresponding images within seconds!

The peg pictures below are the standard pictures that memory geniuses use to visualize numbers. You can either use these images or pick your own for each number. The associations and images that you create with your own imagination will last much longer and will be more effective for you. You may write your own peg words or draw your own peg shapes in the last column. Make them as colourful as possible.

Number	Pegs	Alternate Pegs	Your Own Pegs
0–Donut		football, hula hoop, key ring	
1–Candle		stick, paintbrush, spear	
2–Duck		swan, clothes hanger	
3–Heart		butterfly's wings	
4–Sailboat		playground slide	
5–Seahorse		S hook, snake shaped like 5	

6–Elephant trunk		golf club, hockey stick	
7–Candy cane		axe, boomerang	
8–Snowman		hourglass	
9–Tennis racket		round balloon on a string	
10–Girl + Hula hoop		stick + hoop, bat + ball	

Have you committed each associated picture to mind? Let's do a short recall test. Covering the pictures above, look at the following and write down their corresponding number.

 _  _  _  _

Now that you know the corresponding images to each number, let's see how to use the Number Shape System to peg numbers and words. The first thing to remember is to use the shapes associated with the numbers, not the numbers themselves. Let us assume that your ATM PIN is **5542**. You would remember this number by saying **seahorse seahorse sailboat duck**. Now, can you use the Story Link System to link these four images?

One **seahorse** shoving the other **seahorse** into a speeding **sailboat** overflowing with **ducks**!

You can also use the Pure Link System to link the four images together. Try it here:

Seahorse and seahorse:

_____

_____

Seahorse and sailboat:

_____

_____

Sailboat and duck:

_____

_____

Let's try this method with a list of ten words that need to be remembered.

office, joy, train, shop, flowers,
ocean, cricket, study, car, tree

Now list these words in the order that you would like to remember them, next to each peg.

1. Candle   Office
2. Duck   Joy
3. Heart   Train
4. Sailboat   Shop

5.	Seahorse	Flowers
6.	Elephant's trunk	Ocean
7.	Candy cane	Cricket
8.	Snowman	Study
9.	Tennis racket	Car
10.	Girl hula hooping	Tree

Once this is done, go back to the Link System and link each word to their associated peg.

1. Candle and office: A melting office building made entirely of lit candles.
2. Duck and joy: A mother duck joyfully frolicking with her ducklings.
3. Heart and train: I love trains! Or heart-shaped train tracks.
4. Sailboat and shop: A sailboat crashing into a shop.
5. Seahorse and flowers: A seahorse wearing a tiara of flowers on its head.
6. Elephant's trunk and ocean: A thirsty elephant drinking up all the water in the ocean through its trunk.
7. Candy cane and cricket: Playing cricket using a candy cane instead of a bat.
8. Snowman and study: A snowman studying how to keep cool in the summer.
9. Tennis racket and car: A car in the rain with its tennis-racket-windscreen wipers on.
10. Girl hula-hooping and tree: A tree hula-hooping while balancing a girl on its highest branch.

Now, just by remembering the associations between the words and their pegs, can you remember their correct order? The first one has been done for you. Try to complete the rest using only the peg words as retrieval cues.

Snowman studying: No. <u>8</u>
Elephant drinking ocean water through trunk: No. _____
Seahorse wearing flowers: No. _____
Car with tennis-racket-windscreen wipers: No. _____
Candy cane bat instead of cricket bat: No. _____
Duck joyfully frolicking: No. _____

Pro Tip: Some words such as joy, love, prayer, peace, etc. are abstract words with no concrete images. You will need to conjure up a concrete image for these words or use them as they are in your associations, for example, 'Joyfully frolicking'.

Exercise 1: Properties of Cotton

Using the Number Shape System, learn the physical properties of cotton fibres. The first three have been done for you. The characteristics of cotton fibres are:

1. Uses: Used for spinning, knitting, weaving, dyeing and printing.
2. Colour: Cotton fibre could be white, creamy white, bluish white, yellowish white, or grey.
3. Tensile strength: Cotton is a moderately strong fibre. It is stronger when wet.
4. Elongation at break: Cotton does not stress easily.
5. Elastic recovery: Cotton is a rigid fibre and not elastic.
6. Effect of heat: Cotton has an excellent resistance to degradation by heat. It begins to turn yellow after several hours at 120^0 C.
7. Effect of sunlight: There is a gradual loss of strength when cotton is exposed to sunlight and the fibre gradually turns yellow.
8. Effects of age: Cotton shows very less loss of strength if stored carefully. Even after years of storage, cotton may differ only slightly from new fabrics.

9. Comfort: Comfortable to wear through all seasons.

Candle and uses: Imagine using a candle to spin, knit and weave! The candle is dyed and there is a pattern printed on it.

Duck and colour: A duck that keeps changing colour from white to creamy white to bluish white to yellowish white or even grey!

Heart and tensile strength: A wet heart flexing its strong muscles proudly.

Sailboat and elongation at break:

_____

_____

Seahorse and elastic recovery:

_____

_____

Elephant's trunk and effect of heat:

_____

_____

Candy cane and effect of sunlight:

_____

_____

Snowman and effects of age:

_____

_____

Tennis racket and comfort:

_____

_____

The Number Rhyme System

If you think about it, you already know the Number Rhyme System. Remember your nursery rhymes? Here's one that you will definitely remember.

One, two, buckle my shoe,
Three, four, open the door,
Five, six, pick up the sticks,
Seven, eight, lay them straight,
Nine, ten, a big fat hen!

The Number Rhyme System is very similar to this nursery rhyme. In this method, numbers are represented by images of things that rhyme with each number. The rhyming words are then used as peg words to remember short numbers or a smaller list of items such as to-do lists, recipes, shopping lists, ATM PINs, phone numbers, flight numbers, hotel room numbers, appointment times, birthdays, history timelines, etc. This method is usually used for numbers 0 to 10, but you can come up with your own rhyming words for number 11 and above.

Given below are a list of numbers with their associate pegs or rhyming words and images. While this is a generic list, please feel free to use your own rhyming words that you are more comfortable with.

Number	Pegs	Peg Image	Alternate Pegs	Your Own Pegs
0	Hero		Bureau	
1	Bun		Sun, Nun	
2	Shoe		Zoo, Glue	

3	Tree		Bee, Knee	
4	Door		Floor, Store	
5	Hive		Hard drive	
6	Sticks		Bricks, Ticks	
7	Heaven		Raven, Oven	
8	Gate		Bait, Plate	
9	Wine		Twine, Valentine	
10	Hen		Pen, Den	

Take as much time as you need to memorize the peg words and picture a clear image of the peg words in your mind. Now, let's do a quick recall exercise. Cover the page above and write down the corresponding numbers for the following peg words:

_____   _____   _____   _____   _____   _____

Exercise 2: Remembering Schedules

You have a busy day ahead of you. Here's your schedule: you need to go to work, finish your morning meetings, a few chores, and then catch a flight to New Delhi.

1. 9 a.m.—Fill petrol in car.
2. 10 a.m.—Team meeting.
3. 11 a.m.—Breakfast meeting with a client.
4. 12 p.m.—Return book to the library.
5. 12.30 p.m.—Pickup clothes from laundromat.
6. 2 p.m.—Pick up son from school.
7. 4 p.m.—Print flight tickets.
8. 5 p.m.—Stop at ATM on the way to the airport.
9. 8 p.m.—Flight to Delhi.

In this exercise, since time is in numbers, you do not need to take the serial numbers (1,2,3...) into consideration to list the chores, but you can directly associate the time to the particular task. Since you also have two additional numbers of 11 o'clock and 12 o'clock, take a minute to associate appropriate rhyming words. You can denote '12.30' by adding a 'half' to whatever you rhyme number 12 with. For the purpose of this exercise, you can rhyme 11 to lemon and 12 to shelf. You can picture 12.30 to be one shelf plus another half shelf or another shelf broken in half. Now, you can start the associations with the peg words.

9 a.m.—Fill petrol in car—imagine filling up your car with **wine** instead of petrol.

10 a.m.—Team meeting—a big fat **hen** squawks out the presentation at the team meeting.

11 a.m.—Breakfast meeting with client—imagine you and your client eating breakfast out of a gigantic **lemon**!

12 p.m.—Return book to library—picture the library to be an enormous **shelf** that you need to heave the book into.

12.30 p.m.—Pick up clothes from laundromat—clothes are overflowing from one **shelf** into **half** of the next!

Can you work out the remaining associations?

2 p.m.—Pick up son from school_____
4 p.m.—Print flight tickets_____
5 p.m.—Stop at ATM_____
8 p.m.—Flight to Delhi_____

Now read the following questions and see how fast you can answer them.

1. What should you do at 12.30 p.m.?
2. What do you have scheduled at 11 a.m.?
3. What time do you need to be at the ATM?
4. What time is your flight to Delhi?
5. What should you do at 10 a.m.?

Were you able to visualize the pictures clearly? If you were not able to remember, it could be because:

- You made associations that you did not like.

- The associations were too close or similar to each other.
- There was not enough exaggeration.
- The images that you imagined were not strong enough.
- There was not enough movement.
- The links were too weak or the associations between numbers and their pegs were too weak.
- Perhaps there was not enough humour involved.

Exercise 3

Using either the Number Shape Method or the Number Rhyme Method, try and memorize the following:

1. An ATM PIN number: 8392
2. A friend's address: Apartment 503, Double Road
3. A bank account number: 783630289
4. Where you parked your car at the mall: Lower Basement, parking space 5464
5. Licence plate number of an Uber or Ola cab: 5386
6. A friend's mobile number: 9789055838
7. A credit card number: 8768 9890 1322 4500
8. Shopping list to bake a cake: flour, baking powder, baking soda, unsalted butter, sugar, eggs, vanilla extract and milk.
9. Dates for exams: July 4th, 6th, 10th, 11th, 17th, 20th, 21st, 25th and 28th.
10. Syllabus for an exam: Pages 67, 89, 90, 108, 112 and 118.

The Major System

Take a brief glance at the next two lines and try to memorize them. Now close the book and write down both lines.

CONQUER FROM WITHIN
2393821—9838—192749

Which line were you able to remember better? I bet it was the first one, even though both lines had the same number of characters. Why was it easier to remember the first line better than the second one? Because, even if you did not understand the first line, it still holds more meaning than a random combination of numbers!

When you use the Major System to peg numbers to letters or words, you will be able to remember longer numbers such as your passport number, Aadhaar card number, credit card number, multiple phone numbers, formulae, etc. easily.

In this method, you must first learn a simple phonetic alphabet. Phonetic alphabets are nothing but the sounds that a particular letter makes. For example, instead of saying 't' as in 'tea,' you say 'tuh'; and instead of saying 'n' as in 'en,' you say 'nuh'. If you are worried about learning a whole new phonetic alphabet, it may encourage you to know that you need to learn only ten basic sounds which can be memorized within ten minutes! Just follow the retrieval cues for each sound and you will never forget it!

The basic concept of the system is that it makes use of different consonants or consonant sounds for each number from 0 to 9 using a special code. Here is the list from 0 to 9:

0—s, z, soft c (c with the 'suh' sound as in 'cent')
1—t, d, th
2—n
3—m
4—r
5—l
6—j, sh, ch, soft g (g with the 'juh' sound as in 'general')
7—k, hard c (cuh sound), hard g (guh sound), qu (q has a kuh sound)
8—f, v
9—b, p

Retrieval Cues 1

0—The letter 's' or 'z' is the first sound of the word 'zero' while 'o' is the last letter. The letter 'c' with the 'suh' sound is also used for the number 0.

1—The letters 't' and 'd' have one downward stroke.

2—The letter 'n' has two downward strokes.

3—The letter 'm' has three downward strokes.

4—'Four' in many languages ends with an 'r'. For example, chaar in Hindi, katër in Albanian, vier in Dutch and German, pedwar in Welsh and quarter in Latin.

5—If you hold five fingers up on your left hand, your index finger and thumb form the letter 'L' like ✍. The Roman numeral for number 50 is also L.

6—The mirror image of '6' looks like 'j' and 'g' (pronounced as 'juh').

7—Two number 7s can be used to form the letter 'K'—one 7 right side up and the other, upside down like so ⤨. 'Guh' sounds like 'kuh' and so the letters g, c and q are also used for the number 7.

8—𝓕 in cursive writing, 'f' has two loops just like the number 8. 𝓕 sounds like 'fuh'.

9—'p' and 'b' are the mirror images of number 9.

Retrieval Cue 2

The following phrase will help you remember the letters in the correct sequence:

                1 2 3 4   5 6 7 8 90
          TeN MoRe LoGiC FiBS

Retrieval Cue 3

Make up a ridiculous rhyme with the numbers and their

associated letters and sounds:

One **T**ied his **T**iny **T**oes,
Two **N**early **N**ever **K**nows.
Three **M**elted **M**oney **M**ore,
Four **R**arely **R**eally **R**oared!
Five **L**oved a **L**ittle **L**amp,
Six Wa**s J**ealous of His **J**am.
Seven **K**issed a **K**angaroo
Eight **Fl**ipped His **Fl**utey **F**oo.
Nine **B**ooped a **B**uzzing **B**ee
Zero **Z**igzagged Through the **S**ea.

As with the Number Shape System and the Number Rhyme System, take time to learn the numbers and their associated sounds. Look away from this page and see how many numbers and associated sounds you can remember. Once you remember them in order, test yourself and see if you remember them randomly, out of sequence. Keep repeating the numbers and associated sounds till they are second nature to you, practising everywhere you go. If you see a licence plate number '4737', you should be able to immediately think 'rkmk' or when you see an address '45/13', you should be able to convert it into 'rl/tm' immediately. Also, whenever you see random words in your everyday life, such as store names and words on billboards, etc. you should be able to convert them into numbers. For example, 'Motor Minds' can easily be converted to 314 3210 and Lion Bubble Gum to 52 995 73.

Pro Tips:

- These sounds will **always** be associated with the same numbers.
- **Sounds** of letters are more important than the letters themselves.

- Since only sounds are taken into consideration, silent letters in words are ignored. For example, the 'k' in 'knee, knock and knife' and the 'p' in 'psalm' are ignored.
- Vowels are never used for pegs. Consonants that sound like vowels such as w, h and y are also not used as pegs. For example, 'Buy Now' will be converted to '9 2'!
- Letters that sound alike are used to represent one number. For example, 'v' and 'f' make 'vuh' and 'fuh' sounds that sound alike and represent the number 8.
- Some letters represent different numbers based on their sounds. For example, 'c' as in 'cyst' represents the number 0 while 'c' as in 'carry' represents the number 7. In the same way, 'g' as in 'goat' represents the number 7 while 'g' as in 'gender' represents the number 6.
- Double consonants such as 'tt' 'mm' 'll' are counted as a single consonant since they have the same sound as a single consonant. Therefore, the word 'commitment' is phonetically read as 'comitment' and 'professor' is phonetically read as 'profeser'.
- Double letters pronounced differently in the same word represent two different numbers. For example, 'accept' is pronounced as 'aksept' and 'k' and 's' represent 7 and 0 respectively.
- When there is a word that has a combination of two different letters having the same sound, it is denoted only by one number. For example, the word 'pick' has a 'c' and 'k' which have the 'cuh' sound and, therefore, are denoted with the single number 7 not 77. However, if the same sound has two syllables in the same word, they are represented twice by the same number. For example, peacock is represented as 977. Remember, you only go by the sound of the word not the number of letters it has.

- Words that are made by converting the numbers need not be real words. Made-up words can be used as long as you can remember them. For example, you may not be able to think of a word for the numbers 155, but you can use a made-up word—Taloola—to remember it.
- You can use words from different languages not just English, as long as the sounds are the same for each number. For example, you can convert the number 64 to **chaar** instead of **chair** if you are more comfortable with Hindi.
- In case you cannot make a phrase or sentence with long numbers, use the Link System to visualize linking the words together.

Don't worry if all this sounds confusing. Once you put this system to use, remembering long numbers will be as easy as ABC!

Exercise 4

Since this is an important technique, let's make sure that you are thorough with it. Write down the associated letter sounds for the following numbers. Keep practising till you know it thoroughly.

9 _____ 0 _____ 2 _____ 4 _____ 8 _____ 6 _____

Write down the associated numbers for the following letter sounds

t _____ sh _____ ch _____ k _____ p _____ b
m _____ soft g _____ z _____ v _____ n _____ r

Advancing the Major System of Pegging

So far, we have talked about pegging sounds for numbers from 0 to 9. Now, we will see how to make up a word for any number, no matter how many digits it contains. Throughout this book we will only work on numbers from 0 to 100 but using the same system, challenge yourself to go beyond 100 and see how far you can go.

Using the same phonetic sounds that were used for numbers 0 to 9, you can think of peg words that use the same sounds for each number and then peg those to their respective numbers, this way they will never change. In future, whenever you hear that particular number, you should be able to remember its corresponding peg word. So instead of associating numbers individually to individual sounds, you can take a whole chunk of numbers and associate it with just one word. You can then use the peg word in association with anything else in order to remember long sequences of numbers such as credit card numbers, all the elements in the periodic table along with their atomic numbers, and even the value of pi to its 100th decimal place or more!

As with other techniques, it will initially take you a little time and effort to peg each number to its phonetic word, but once you get the hang of it, you will be able to rattle off long sequences of numbers in their correct order, without giving it a second thought! Practice is the key.

Let's begin with the numbers that you already know. You know that the sounds associated with '0' are 's' and 'z' so, an appropriate peg word for '0' that has only these sounds may be 'his' or 'hiss'. Remember, since the consonants 'w', 'h' and 'y' are treated like vowels and are not counted as sounds, 'his' or 'hiss' will denote the number '0.' This word will now, always be associated with the number '0.' So if you see a 0 anywhere, the word that needs to pop into your mind immediately is 'his' or 'hiss'. You can pick what you are comfortable with.

In the same way, the number 1 is represented by the sounds that 't' and 'd' make. You can add in additional sounds of 'th' and 'dh' since they sound similar. Now, think of a word that has just one 't' or 'd' or 'th' or 'dh' sound. For now, you can use the word 'tie'. If you translate the word 'tie' into numbers, it is denoted by the number 1. So from now on, the word 'tie' will always be used to denote the number 1.

The number 2 is represented by the 'n' sound and you can have words such as now, no, know, etc. You can also use names such as Noah to denote a number. Avoid concepts such as 'now' or 'know', but use concrete words. Here, 'Noah' can depict 'Noah's ark.'

Moving on to two-digit numbers, the number 11 has two 1s and therefore, the word that you use needs to have two sounds of 't' or 'd' or 'th'. How about 'tot'? You can also use the following words—tit, tat, tut, that, thud, dad, did, dud, etc.

The number 12 has a 1 and 2 and therefore, you can use the associated sounds for the numbers 1 and 2 which are 't, d, th, dh and n'. Therefore, you can represent the number 12 by words such as den, ten, then, tin, din, thin, etc.

Let's work out the numbers from 0 to 100. You may not be comfortable with the associated words used in this book, but you are welcome to write your own words. If you are comfortable with a different language, you are free to use words of that language— just make sure to use the correct sounds of 's, t, n, m, r, l, j, k, f' and 'b' (and similar sounds of 'd, c', etc.) to denote the numbers 0, 1, 2, 3, 4, 5, 6, 7, 8 and 9 respectively.

Number	Peg Word	Your own word
0	Hiss	
1	Tie	
2	Noah	
3	Ma	
4	Row	
5	Law	
6	Jaw	

7	Cow	
8	Foe	
9	Bee	
10	Toes	
11	Tot	
12	Den	
13	Tin	
14	Tire	
15	Toll (Booth)	
16	Taj (Mahal)	
17	Tick	
18	Dove	
19	Tub	
20	Nose	
21	Net	
22	Nun	
23	Numb (num)	
24	Henry	
25	Nail	
26	Nudge	
27	Neck	
28	Knife	
29	Nib	
30	Moose	
31	Mat	
32	Man	
33	Mom	
34	More	
35	Mule	
36	Match	

37	Mickey	
38	Movie	
39	Map	
40	Rice	
41	Rod	
42	Run	
43	Rain	
44	Roar	
45	Rail	
46	Raja	
47	Rock	
48	Roof	
49	Robe	
50	Lace	
51	Loot	
52	Loony	
53	Lamb (lam)	
54	Leer	
55	Lolly	
56	Leash	
57	Lake	
58	Laugh (laf)	
59	Lap	
60	Juice	
61	Jut	
62	Chain	
63	Chime	
64	Chore	
65	Jail	
66	Judge (juj)	

67	Joke	
68	Chef	
69	Job	
70	Case	
71	Cut	
72	Acorn	
73	Come	
74	Car	
75	Coal	
76	Cage	
77	Cake	
78	Café	
79	Cup	
80	Fuss	
81	Feet	
82	Fan	
83	Fame	
84	Fire	
85	Fall	
86	Fudge (fuj)	
87	Fish	
88	Five	
89	Fab	
90	Bus	
91	Bat	
92	Bun	
93	Bomb (bom)	
94	Bar	
95	Ball	
96	Barge (baj)	

97	**Buck**	
98	**Barf (baf)**	
99	**Puff**	
100	**Daisies**	

Yes, this long list does look a little daunting but since you now have the basic concept, even if you were to forget the peg word, you can just put the sounds of numbers together and remember it. For example, if you forget the peg word for the number 98, you know that 9 has the sound 'b' and 8 has the sound 'f' so if you put the two sounds together (bf), you should be able to remember the word 'barf'.

Exercise 5: Converting Numbers to Words and Words to Numbers

As mentioned earlier, this is an important memory system which can be used to memorize long numbers in mathematics, the periodic table, addresses, telephone numbers, Aadhaar card numbers and just about any number that you require on a day-to-day basis so it helps to be thorough with this system. Try and work out the following questions. You can either use the words listed above or think of your own words. Remember, it is the sound of the letters that is important, not the words themselves.

Convert the following numbers into their letters and then into words. Try not to refer to the list above.

	Number	Letters	Words
1.	89	_____	_____
2.	20	_____	_____
3.	99	_____	_____
4.	29	_____	_____
5.	76	_____	_____

6.	56	_____	_____
7.	19	_____	_____
8.	93	_____	_____
9.	100	_____	_____
10.	38	_____	_____
11.	0	_____	_____
12.	11	_____	_____
13.	91	_____	_____
14.	26	_____	_____
15.	44	_____	_____
16.	58	_____	_____
17.	14	_____	_____
18.	82	_____	_____
19.	80	_____	_____
20.	77	_____	_____
21.	3	_____	_____
22.	66	_____	_____
23.	71	_____	_____
24.	52	_____	_____
25.	1	_____	_____

Now convert the following words into their letters and then the letters into their respective numbers. Don't forget that vowels and the letters 'w', 'h' and 'y' are not counted in this system and, therefore, do not have associated numbers.

	Words	**Letters**	**Numbers**
1.	Try	_____	_____
2.	Bus	_____	_____

3.	Match	_____	_____
4.	Row	_____	_____
5.	Noah	_____	_____
6.	Daisies	_____	_____
7.	Raja	_____	_____
8.	Robe	_____	_____
9.	Jaw	_____	_____
10.	Moose	_____	_____
11.	Lace	_____	_____
12.	The	_____	_____
13.	Cake	_____	_____
14.	Chef	_____	_____
15.	Acorn	_____	_____
16.	Chime	_____	_____
17.	Juice	_____	_____
18.	Loot	_____	_____
19.	Nail	_____	_____
20.	Taj	_____	_____
21.	Map	_____	_____
22.	Toes	_____	_____
23.	Fish	_____	_____
24.	Mule	_____	_____
25.	Nun	_____	_____

Exercise 6: Converting Longer Numbers and Words

Let us try the same thing with longer numbers and words. Write down the associated numbers for each word in the first column and make up your own words using the pegs in the second column. The first word is worked out for you. Possible answers are given below but try to work it out on your own.

Shelf	—	658		614	—	**Ashtray**
1. Kettle	—	_____	1.	954	—	_____
2. Crown	—	_____	2.	9491	—	_____
3. Table	—	_____	3.	7212	—	_____
4. Cigar	—	_____	4.	692	—	_____
5. Couple	—	_____	5.	344	—	_____
6. Shelter	—	_____	6.	915	—	_____
7. Kneepad	—	_____	7.	1540	—	_____
8. Paper	—	_____	8.	4210	—	_____
9. Basket	—	_____	9.	0137	—	_____
10. Trolley	—	_____	10.	741	—	_____

Possible Answers

1. 715	6. 6514	1. Blare	6. Battle
2. 742	7. 291	2. Parapet	7. Dollars
3. 195	8. 994	3. Canteen	8. Runts
4. 074	9. 1207	4. Japan	9. Stomach
5. 795	10. 145	5. Mirror	10. Carrot

THE ALPHABET PEG SYSTEM

The Alphabet Peg System has two systems—Familiar Peg Words and the Alphabet Rhyme System. These two systems can be used to remember random alphabets such as PNR numbers, alphanumeric passwords, formulae and long lists of words.

Familiar Peg Words

Remember how you learnt the alphabet in kindergarten? A for apple, B for ball, C for cat, etc. Well, this is exactly how the alphabet peg system works. Here, instead of numbers, you use letters A–Z and use their associated words to remember lists that have more than ten items. Here's a list of familiar associated words that you may have grown up with. You can either use these words or use words that you are more comfortable with.

Alphabet	Peg Word	Your Own Word
A	Apple	_____
B	Ball	_____
C	Cat	_____
D	Dog	_____
E	Egg	_____
F	Frog	_____
G	Grass	_____
H	Hat	_____
I	Ink	_____
J	Jam	_____
K	Kite	_____
L	Leaf	_____
M	Monkey	_____
N	Nose	_____
O	Oar	_____
P	Parrot	_____
Q	Queen	_____
R	Rope	_____
S	Sun	_____

T	Tap	_____
U	Umbrella	_____
V	Violin	_____
W	Well	_____
X	X-ray	_____
Y	Yacht	_____
Z	Zebra	_____

Pro Tips:

- You do not have to link the first word to the second word. Just remembering the peg word should be enough for you to recall the associated word. For example, you do not have to link rainbow to sunflower. However, just remembering the peg word 'apple' should be enough for you to visualize a 'rainbow-coloured apple' which should lead you to the word to be remembered—rainbow.
- Since you already know 'apple', 'ball' and 'cat' in order, you will automatically remember all the associated words in order.
- Don't spend too long creating these images. Just visualize them and immediately move on to the next item on the list.
- If there are more than twenty-six words to be remembered, make associations for the first twenty-six words till you reach Z, then start over from A and link a second object to the first image. For example, if the 27th word is 'bat', you need to link **apple** with **rainbow** as well as **bat**, so you can visualize batting a rainbow-coloured apple.

Exercise 7: Familiar Peg Words

Using Familiar Peg Words, try to remember the following list of twenty-six random words:

> rainbow, sunflower, fish, window, car, dice, football,
> shirt, tomatoes,
> balloon, sunglasses, hammer, lotus, eggs, table,
> butterfly, roof, tree,
> books, piano, shampoo, handbag, classroom, stapler,
> brinjal, bottle

First, pair each word to their peg words. So, rainbow will be paired with apple, sunflower will be paired with ball, fish will be paired with cat, etc. Once the words are paired, start your associations as you have done in the previous exercises. Remember to visualize the associations clearly. Once you have completed this exercise, close the book and see if you can remember all twenty-six words without looking.

Apple and rainbow: Imagine an apple that is multi coloured like the rainbow.

Ball and sunflower: Imagine throwing and catching a sunflower instead of a ball.

Cat and fish: A fish whacking a cat's nose with its tail.

Dog and window: A dog jumping through a window only to hit its nose on the glass.

Egg and car: Imagine driving an egg instead of a car.

Can you do the rest?

Frog and dice_____

Grass and football _____

Hat and shirt_____

Ink and tomatoes _____

Jam and balloon _____

Kite and sunglasses _____

Leaf and hammer _____

Monkey and lotus_____

Nose and eggs _____

Oar and table _____

Parrot and butterfly _____

Queen and roof _____

Rope and tree _____

Sun and books_____

Tap and piano_____

Umbrella and shampoo _____

Violin and handbag _____

Well and classroom_____

X-ray and stapler _____

Yacht and brinjal _____

Zebra and bottle _____

Alphabet Rhyme System

This system of memory is exactly like the Number Rhyme System, except in this case rhyming words are used for the alphabet instead of numbers. This system can also be used to remember long lists, speeches and study material. Given below is a list of generic rhyming words that memory experts use, but please feel free to use words that you are more comfortable with.

Letter	Peg Rhyming Word	Your Own Word
A	Hay	_____
B	Bee	_____
C	Sea	_____
D	Deer	_____
E	Knee	_____

Letter	Peg Rhyming Word	Your Own Word
F	Effort	_____
G	Jeans	_____
H (hetch)	Age	_____
I	Eye	_____
J	Jay (bird)	_____
K	Cake	_____
L	Shell	_____
M	Hem	_____
N	Hen	_____
O	Oak	_____
P	Pea	_____
Q	Cue (snooker)	_____
R	Arm	_____
S	Snake (hiss)	_____
T	Tea	_____
U	Ewe	_____
V	Veal	_____
W (double u)	Bubble	_____
X	Eggs	_____
Y	Wire	_____
Z	Zen	_____

Now using the associated words as peg words, you can memorize a long list or even a speech! Let's try the following exercise.

Exercise 8: Remembering Passwords

a) You work in a bank and you get a high security password every day. The password is generally alphanumeric and you

need to use the same password through the day. Using the Alphabet Rhyme System, how would you remember it?
Password—**sjPd3a7**

Step 1—First convert the password into its associated peg words.
s—snake
j—jay (bird)
P—PEA
d—deer
3—heart (number shape)
a—hay
7—candy cane (number shape)

Step 2—Use the Story Link Method to link the words.

A **snake** and a **jay bird** are fighting over a huge **PEA** when along comes a **deer** with a **heart**-shaped **hay** hat on its head and offers them a **candy cane** instead.

Since the P needs to be in capitals, you can imagine it to be HUGE.

You can also use the Pure Link System to remember your password.

Snake and jay bird_____

Jay bird and pea_____

Pea and deer_____

Deer and heart_____

Heart and hay_____

Hay and candy cane_____

b) Password—**xkCos9s1v**

Step 1—Convert

x   ___   _____

k	—	_____
C	—	_____
o	—	_____
s	—	_____
9	—	_____
S	—	_____
1	—	_____
v	—	_____

Step 2—Story Link_____

_____

_____

Exercise 9: Remembering Formulae

Using any of the Alphabet Peg Systems, try to remember the following formulae. Hint: you can either remember symbols like +, −, x, %, etc. as they are or you can assign specific peg words to them. + can be an ambulance, − can be a magic wand, x can be an X that marks the spot, = can be train tracks, etc. The key, as always, is to use your imagination.

    a)   Area of a Trapezoid $A = \frac{1}{2} \times h \times (a+b)$

Where:
    A is the area
    h is the perpendicular height
    a is the short base
    b is the long base

Step 1—Convert

A	—	_____
½	—	_____

h   __   _____

a   __   _____

b   __   _____

Step 2—Story Link _____

_____

_____

    b)   Converting celsius to fahrenheit formula:
        $F = C \times 9/5 + 32$

Step 1—Convert

Hint: Use the Number Shape System and the Major System to convert the numbers.

F   __   _____

C   __   _____

9   __   _____

5   __   _____

32   __   _____

Step 2—Story Link _____

_____

_____

SUMMARY

- The Peg System uses an established list of words and images to act as pegs on which you can 'hang' new information. These words never change and are always associated with the corresponding number or letter of the alphabet.
- New information is 'hung' on pegs by associating and visualizing them with the pre-determined words.
- Pegging helps you remember items in their correct order. It also helps you remember the item's exact position on the list.
- Once the words to be remembered are pegged to the alphabet, you can use the Pure Link System or the Story Link System to link the words.

The Number Peg System

The Number Shape System

- Uses images that have a similar shape to their corresponding numbers.
- Uses numbers 0 to 9 and so can be used for short lists of ten items or less. However, you can combine the shapes for numbers greater than 10.

The Number Rhyme System

- Uses images that rhyme with their corresponding numbers.
- Uses numbers 0 to 10 and can be used for short lists of eleven items or less. However, you can extend it by making up your own rhymes for numbers eleven and above.

The Major System

- This system uses a phonetic alphabet, which is a combination of sounds to represent specific numbers.
- Converts numbers to corresponding letters, which you can then make into words by adding vowels.

- This system helps you remember very long numbers and is virtually limitless in the amount of information you can remember since any number, no matter how large, can be converted into its corresponding letters.

The Alphabet Peg System

- The Alphabet Peg System pegs specific words to each letter of the alphabet.
- This method can be used to remember long lists, PNR numbers, flight numbers, passwords and formulae.

The Familiar Peg Words System

- Pegs familiar words to specific letters of the alphabet.

The Alphabet Rhyme System

- Pegs words that rhyme with the letters of the alphabet.

Chapter 6

Memory Techniques

PART FOUR: JOURNEYS, NICKNAMES AND MIND MAPS

The Journey Method

> *Magnussen, 'The Appledore vaults are my Mind Palace.*
> *You know about Mind Palaces, don't you, Sherlock? How*
> *to store information so you never forget it—by picturing it.*
> *I just sit here, I close my eyes...and down*
> *I go to my vaults. I can go anywhere inside*
> *my vaults...my memories...'*

SHERLOCK, 'HIS LAST VOW' (2014)

The Journey Method is an ancient method of memory that is over 2,000 years old. It was used by the Romans and Greeks much before paper was invented and more recently, by Sherlock Holmes. The Journey Method is also called the Method of Loci (locations), the Mind Palace, the Memory Palace and the Roman Room. It is a simple method of using landmarks along a familiar route such as the route from your home to your school or a route even within your own home, to remember information. You simply 'place' the information to be remembered on a familiar peg that you know well. Since it is a familiar peg, remembering it will automatically recall the associated information.

Location provides you with a coherent context that gives

some meaning to the information that you are studying. It also helps you remember two pieces of similar information simply by 'placing' them in different locations so that you do not get confused between them. It combines the Link Method and Peg Systems to associate new information to something that is well-known and familiar. It is a simple yet extremely powerful technique to remember long or large pieces of information and can be used to memorize long speeches, stories, formulae, poems, shopping lists, names of presidents or prime ministers in correct order, periodic table, key points to long answers, etc. Since each journey is a different location, one list remembered using this technique can be easily distinguished from another, even if there are overlapping items.

Everybody uses locations as memory tools, knowingly or unknowingly. If you were asked what you had for breakfast this morning, you would immediately picture yourself eating at your dining table (location) or the sofa or maybe even your bed, before focussing on what exactly you were eating. If you picture information without its surrounding context, you would only see that bit of information floating in air and it would be meaningless to you. But if you give it some context (dining table, sofa, or bed), then you would add a background to it, thereby making that information a bit more meaningful and easy to remember.

The Route Journey Method

The Route Journey Method takes you on a journey from one place to another, marking certain landmarks along the way. For example, picture the route that you take from your home to your school every day. Now, what is the first landmark that you see when you step outside your front door? It may be your front gate. Use your front door as the first landmark and the front gate as your second. After you leave your front gate, what do you see? A large tree? Great. Use that as your third landmark. Once you pass the tree, you may see a bakery. Use that as your fourth landmark. After you pass the bakery, you need to stop at a traffic light. Use the traffic light as your fifth landmark. Now that the signal has changed, you turn right and now you are passing a petrol bunk. Use that as your sixth landmark...and so on, till you reach your final landmark—your classroom.

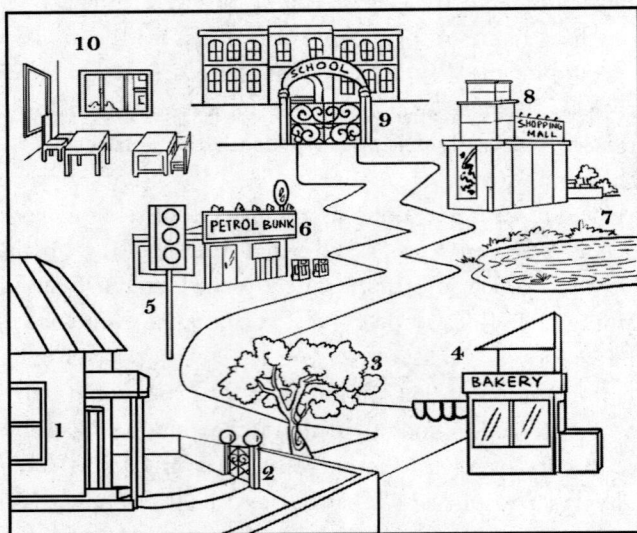

Once you have this route and its landmarks firmly fixed in your mind, you are ready to start using this technique to store further information that you may need to remember in sequence (or not). Simply associate the information that you want to remember to each landmark along the way from your home to your school. Here, the landmarks act as pegs since they will never change. All you have to do is hang whatever you need to remember on these pegs and go on a journey from your home to your school while remembering each piece of information at each landmark. Just by picturing the landmark, you should be able to remember its associated memory.

For example, the following is the list of landmarks from your home to your school along with a list of what you need to do today.

	Route	To-Do List
1.	Front door of house	Homework
2.	Front gate	Group study
3.	Tree	Basketball practice
4.	Bakery	Fill up petrol in bike
5.	Traffic light	Go to tailor for measurements
6.	Petrol bunk	Singing practice
7.	Lake	Chemistry tuition
8.	Shopping mall	Pick up laundry
9.	Front gate of school	Get watch repaired
10.	Desk in classroom	Buy milk on the way home

You certainly have a busy day today! How will you remember all your chores without writing them down? Simple. Just picture your route from home to school clearly in your mind, seeing all ten landmarks distinctly. Now associate each item to each landmark in the order that you would like to do them. So, front door gets associated with homework, front gate gets related to group study, tree gets linked to basketball practice and so on. Let's work out this exercise below.

Front door—Homework: Your front door is made of huge sheets of paper that you are writing your homework on.

Front gate—Group study: Your study group is sitting around the front gate, lobbing information back and forth over it.

Tree—Basketball practice: Imagine jumping high up over the tree to dunk your basketball.

Bakery—Fill up petrol in bike: Your bike is faint with thirst and so it coughs and sputters all the way to the bakery for some refreshing petrol.

Traffic light—Tailor for measurements: The traffic light is made up of measuring tape and red, orange and green buttons and pins.

Petrol bunk—Singing practice _____

Lake—Chemistry tuition _____

Shopping mall—Pick up laundry _____

Front gate of school—Get watch repaired _____

Your desk at school—Buy milk _____

The Room Journey Method

The Room Journey Method is also called Memory Palace or Mind Palace. In this method, you simply use the objects in a particular room or many rooms as pegs for what you need to remember. Picture this: You enter your home. The first room is the living room. Look at the room from left to right. As soon as you enter, you have a shoe rack to your left. A little past the shoe rack is a sofa. Beyond the sofa is a bookshelf next to which is the TV set. Next to the TV is a shelf for DVDs and to your right is a settee. So, within your living room itself you have pegs such as:

1. Shoe rack
2. Sofa
3. Bookshelf
4. TV set
5. DVD shelf
6. Settee

Since the living room has only six items that you can use as pegs, you can journey to the next room if you want to remember a list that is more than six items long. The next room is your bedroom. As soon as you enter to the left, is the light switch. Next to that is your study table. Opposite you is your bed and next to that is your mirror. To your right, you have a cupboard. So, in your bedroom, you now have:

7. Light switch
8. Study table
9. Bed
10. Mirror
11. Cupboard

Now if you want to remember more than eleven words, move to the next room which is the kitchen and peg items there. As soon as you enter the kitchen, you have the sink to your immediate left.

The microwave oven is placed further up. The stove is opposite you and to the right of the stove you have the garbage bin and the fridge. So, in the kitchen you have:

12. Sink
13. Microwave oven
14. Stove
15. Garbage bin
16. Fridge

If you need to remember more than sixteen items, go to the next room and peg objects there. Once you can picture the layout of your home with all its objects in each room firmly in your mind, you are ready to start remembering lists, speeches, etc., by using these objects as pegs to hang your information on.

Exercise 1: Geography—Six Physical Divisions of India

Using the above room landmarks, try to remember the six physical divisions of India.

1. The Great Mountain Wall of the North
2. The Great Northern Plains
3. The Great Peninsular Plateau
4. The Great Indian Desert
5. The Coastal Plains
6. The Island Groups

Now, place each of these at the first six landmarks in the living room. Once this is done, start your associations.

1.	The shoe rack	The Great Northern Wall of the North
2.	Sofa	The Great Northern Plains
3.	Bookshelf	The Great Peninsular Plateau
4.	TV set	The Great Indian Desert

5. DVD shelf   The Coastal Plains
6. Settee   The Island Groups

1. Shoe Rack and the Great Northern Wall of the North: Picture entering your house. You're about to keep your shoes in the shoe rack when there is a shuddering earthquake, the whole house begins to shake and suddenly, there's a massive mountain wall growing below your feet taking you higher and higher till you can touch the clouds.

2. Sofa and the Great Northern Plains: You then get on your sofa and slide down the mountain into lush green plains.

3. Bookshelf and the Great Peninsular Plateau: You move on to your bookshelf but it has now become an upside-down triangle (the shape of a plateau).

4. TV set and the Great Indian Desert _____

5. DVD shelf and the Coastal Plains _____

6. Settee and the Island Groups _____

Now, if anybody asks you if you know the physical characteristics of India, simply walk through your living room picturing each characteristic on each landmark and you should be able to remember them all.

The Body Journey Method

This journey method helps you remember words by using parts of your own body as pegs and associating each part with the information that needs to be remembered. Starting from your head to your toes, you have:

1. Hair
2. Face

3. Neck
4. Shoulders
5. Chest
6. Hands
7. Stomach
8. Hips
9. Knees
10. Feet

These are the basic body parts, but if you want to remember information that is longer than ten items, you can use other parts of your body such as your:

11. Eyebrows
12. Eyes
13. Nose
14. Mouth
15. Left hand
16. Right hand
17. Left leg
18. Right leg

Now, all you need to do is peg information to these body parts and you are good to go!

Exercise 2: Geography—South Indian States

Using any of the journey methods, try to remember the states of South India. Hint: use an image of something that you associate with a particular state and place that image on your landmarks. For example, an image of lush green coconut trees can symbolize Kerala.

1.	Andhra Pradesh	3.	Telangana
2.	Karnataka	4.	Puducherry

5.	Kerala	7.	Lakshadweep
6.	Tamil Nadu		

Pro Tips:

- Use familiar locations. Always move in the same direction (preferably left to right).
- Before you start memorizing, plan the route so that you can repeat the same journey without missing any of the landmarks. Be thorough with your route. Make sure it is a route that is personal to you so that it is more familiar.
- You can walk through your house and peg objects. However, it is better to use what you already remember since this is stored in your long-term memory.
- There is no limit to how many pegs you create and therefore this system can be used for remembering long lists, speeches, monologues, poems, etc.
- Make sure you create a strong link between the landmarks and the information that needs to be remembered.
- Landmarks such as door, gate, etc., might seem like mundane objects, but make sure you enhance them in your mind, give them some character or personality which makes them unforgettable.
- Make sure the journey follows a logical path. This will help you remember the correct sequence of items on your list.
- In case you cannot remember an item on your list, it may be because you did not make a strong enough association with the landmark. Don't forget to make colourful, vivid, or ridiculous associations between the landmark and information to be remembered.
- Using this method, you can remember the list in its correct sequence (by journeying from your front door to your desk), reverse sequence (journeying from your desk to your front

door) or from any point (starting at the petrol bunk instead of your front door). In this way, you will be able to remember a speech forwards and backwards and from any point in the middle.

- Keep making your journey longer and longer to remember more information.

- Journeys can be made using any routes—routes from home to school, routes within a building such as your home, local supermarket, school, shopping mall, etc. and route on your own body.

- To store information that you only need for a few hours (shopping lists, to-do lists), you can use the same room or route that you always use but replace or rewrite new information over old information. Once you have finished shopping, you can mentally remove these images from their landmarks, leaving the landmark empty and ready to use again.

- To store information for a longer period of time (periodic table, poems, speeches, formulae), reserve a specific journey for that piece of information only and make the journey appropriate to that subject matter. Review that journey and associated information from time to time so that you do not forget it but do not use the same route for any other information.

Nickname Method

'We called our computer teacher "Spaceman" because he used to walk around the school with his helmet on all the time.'

'We called our history teacher "Fountain" because she lisped and sprayed the front row with her spit while she was teaching.'

'We called Mrs Manuel "Manny" because she was so manly. Also, it was a short form of her name.'

'Bhuvaneshuvari was too long a name to use, and so we just called her "Boo".'

'I call her "Tutu" although it's not her real name because when she was little, she used to ask for two-two of everything!'

How many of you have nicknames or special names for your friends or siblings? How many of you have naughty names for your teachers? Do you have a special name for your best friend? You may come up with nicknames for people based on their physical features, their existing names, some strange mannerisms that they may have or even based on their jobs. Sometimes, if you have two or more classmates with the same name, you might assign a nickname to them to distinguish one from the other. For example, Small Divya, Mousy Ayesha (she was the quiet Ayesha), Four-eyed Debby (she wore glasses), Metal Mouth Sandy (she had braces), etc.

Assigning nicknames to people helps you remember them better. You can apply the same technique of assigning nicknames to study material that you want to remember. Using this naming system, you can learn names of countries along with their capitals, currencies, economies, etc. You can remember authors and their books, inventors and their inventions, and in fact, any kind of information that you want! Just remember to apply the basic rules of visualization, imagination, association and location to the information that you would like to remember as this will make it more concrete in your mind.

Let's look at the following countries and see how we can break up their names to remember them better.

Country	Nickname	Association
Iceland	Ice Land	A land full of ice.
Portugal	Port + Gul	A sea gull circling a port.
Austria	Ostrich + Tree + Ah	Look at that ostrich climbing that tree! Aaah!
Denmark	Den + Mark	Mark the Den with chalk marks.
Czech Republic	Check Republic	✓ Republic
Slovenia	Sloth + Vein + Ya	Sloth getting an injection on his veins, ya!
Canada	Can + Add + Da	Can you add, da?
Switzerland	Itz + er + land	It's a land!
Ireland	fire + land	Burning land of fire!

Pro Tips:

- Break up the word into smaller words or similar sounding words. For example, Germany can be broken up into two words i.e. Germ—many and Australia can be broken up into a similar *sounding* word i.e. ostrich.
- Assign images to all words, whether they are abstract or concrete words. If the word is an abstract word such as 'honest', (hoe-nest) you can picture a concrete image like a garden hoe inside a nest. Do not picture another abstract word.
- Use symbols for abstract words to make them more concrete. For example, 'love' can be denoted by a ♥, 'search' can be denoted by ⚲, 'attracted' can be denoted by ↷, and so on.

- Sometimes, instead of thinking of the word itself, you can think of something that you usually associate with that word. For example, if you are thinking of Egypt, you can replace the word Egypt with an image of a pyramid.
- Make your associations personal. If you have actually visited a place that you are learning about, use the visual images that you experienced instead of thinking up new associated images. Since you have actually had experiences there, your memories would be that much stronger. For example, if you have visited the temples at Mahabalipuram, you do not have to break up the word 'maha-ball-put-ram' and think of associations like a 'huge (maha) ball put on a ram' but you can just cast your mind back to your trip and remember something that stood out for you—maybe one of the temples carved from a single rock—to signify the place.

Let's try to remember the following countries and their currencies.

		Nickname	Association
Country Currency	Denmark Krone	Den + Mark Crone (old lady)	Old crone sitting in her den, putting a mark on her money.
Country Currency	Aruba Florin	Arrow bow Flowering	A bow shooting an arrow through a flowering plant.
Country Currency	Albania Lek	All + Ban Lake	All lakes are banned.
Country Currency	Armenia Dram	Ar + men Dam	Are men dammed?
Country Currency	Bangladesh Taka	Bangles + Desh Take	A country (desh) where you can take bangles

Exercise 3: Inventors and Their Inventions

Let's now try the nickname technique to link inventors to their inventions. The first two have been done for you.

		Nickname	Association
Inventors	Thomas Edison	Edi-son	Son of Edi with a brilliant
Inventions	Lightbulb	Lightbulb	lightbulb over his head.
Inventors	Alexander	Gray-ham	A gray-coloured ham with
	Graham Bell	Bell	a bell around its neck
Inventions	Telephone	Telephone	saying hellooooo into a
			telephone
Inventors	Mary Anderson		
Inventions	Windshield wiper blade		
Inventors	Benjamin Franklin		
Inventions	Bifocal glasses		
Inventors	James Naismith		
Inventions	Basketball (game)		

Exercise 4: Countries and Their Capitals

Using the nickname technique, link the following countries to their capitals.

		Nickname	Association
Country	Bulgaria	Bull	Bull jumping on your sofa.
Capital	Sofia	Sofa	
Country	Switzerland	It's a land	
Capital	Berne	Burn	
Country	New Zealand		
Capital	Wellington		

Country	Romania		
Capital	Bucharest		
Country	Nepal		
Capital	Kathmandu		
Country	India		
Capital	New Delhi		
Country	North Korea		
Capital	Pyongyang		
Country	Uruguay		
Capital	Montevideo		
Country	Indonesia		
Capital	Jakarta		
Country	Philippines		
Capital	Manila		
Country	Afghanistan		
Capital	Kabul		

Pro Tips:

- Feel free to use your own regional languages to break up words. For example, Bangladesh can be broken into Bangles + Desh (country), Lal Bahadur Shastri can be directly translated to 'Red Brave' man.
- Use symbolic images when it is difficult to break up a word. For example, Switzerland is difficult to break up so you can use images that are generally associated with the country such as Swiss army knives, chocolates, watches, cheese, etc.
- To remember the list itself, you can use the journey method. For example, to remember the list of inventors, you can picture each inventor at a particular landmark in your journey. If you are using the Route Journey technique, picture Thomas Edison (Son of Edi with a brilliant lightbulb

over his head) at the front door (first landmark), Alexander Graham Bell (A gray-coloured ham with a bell around its neck saying hellooooo into a telephone) at your front gate (second landmark), etc.

- This technique can help you remember a whole host of connected information. For example, the capital of Bulgaria is Sofia. It is bordered by Romania, Serbia, Macedonia, Greece, Turkey and the Black Sea. Picture a bull (Bulgaria) jumping on a sofa (Sofia) surrounded by a manic arrow (Ro-mania), a surfing bee (Ser-bia) with a big mac on its head (Mac-head-on-ya), Zeus (Greek god) and a turkey—all of them are trying their best not to fall into the Black Sea (Black sea and Turkey are self-describing images).

Mind Maps

This is an unconventional technique that helps you visualize and organize ideas so that you can understand your study material better. Most of the memory techniques that have been discussed so far only aid memory but do not help in understanding information. Mind mapping not only helps you understand what you learn but it also helps you see the information as a whole as well as its connection to other information. The technique of mind mapping is an effective combination of a memory aid and a thinking tool and therefore helps with understanding as well.

In everything that you study, whether you attend a lecture or study for an exam, you rely on your notes for information. Mind mapping is nothing but a more effective way of taking down notes so that you get all your information on one page. It helps you sketch out key ideas during a lecture and see quickly and clearly how each idea relates to each other. It also helps you put all your ideas and information together in one place in order to remember them better.

All this may sound complicated but it is one of the simplest methods to help you study. You simply need to map out your study material and write it down or draw it in a creative way. Information is noted, not word for word or sentence by sentence, but rather in the form of a diagram with lines branching out from one fact to another. Which would you remember better? A photograph or a thousand-word essay describing something? The photograph, of course! This is exactly what a mind map is—representing your study material in a more pictorial way.

Why You Need Mind Maps:

- Mind maps help you concentrate on key points and provide a quick reference for revision before an exam.
- Mind maps can give you an overview of a large subject, at a glance.
- It encourages and strengthens associations.
- The combination of words and images with colours helps you remember the information better. Even if you use only colours to code your sub-branches and not images, you will be able to remember it better than your notes.
- It combines both left and right brain thinking, which means that you will remember it better than if it was just lines of words.
- Since it is your own interpretation of your study material, you will understand it better.
- It helps you map out your thoughts and assists you to brainstorm different ideas to work out a solution to a problem.
- Mind maps use all the functions of visualization, imagination, association and location thus enhancing your memory to its full potential.

How to make a mind map:

1. Start with a blank sheet of paper, preferably A4 or A3 in size and unruled. Turn it sideways (landscape).

2. Write down the main topic or the key word at the centre of the page. This can also be a diagram or image of the central topic that you are studying.

3. From the central figure or key word, draw branches radiating in different directions to signify subheadings.

4. Add sub-branches radiating from these branches to show subheadings of each branch. Again, these are drawn or labelled in different colours.

5. Be sure to make your branches curved and not as straight lines. Curved lines encourage creative thinking.

6. Every time you add another word or image, draw a branch from the key words to connect with it. No matter how many branches you create, it should be possible to journey back along those branches to reach the centre.

7. Label the branches and sub-branches clearly and make sure that the images represent the subject matter clearly.

8. Branches or sub-branches may interconnect, depending on the strength of associations between them. Use arrows to connect linking ideas.

9. Make your map as colourful and beautiful as possible. You can use colours as themes as well, to differentiate one branch or sub-branch from another. Colour helps with clarity. It also helps you recognize chunks of information by colour coding different bits of information and highlights important points.

Exercise 1: Mind Map of Memory Techniques

Let's make a Mind Map of all the memory techniques that we have studied in this book so far in chapters 3, 4, 5 and 6. While this exercise is worked out at the end of this chapter, follow the steps below and try to do the Mind Map by yourself. It may help you to go through the main headings and subheadings of the chapters to get an idea of what to write or draw in your Mind Map.

Step 1—Take an A4 size paper and turn it sideways (landscape).

Step 2—Write 'Memory Techniques' as the heading in the middle of the sheet. If you would like to represent 'memory techniques' with a drawing or a symbol, you're welcome to do so.

Step 3—Now, since you are taking four chapters into consideration, draw four lines branching outwards from the title 'Memory Techniques'. Label the first branch as 'Fun Memory Techniques', the second branch as 'Linking', the third branch as 'Pegging', and the fourth branch as 'Journeys, Nicknames and Mind Maps'. Make all these branches red in colour to show that these are main headings.

Step 4—From the first branch, Fun Memory Techniques, draw five branches and label them 'Acronyms', 'Acrostics', 'Rhymes and Music', 'Number Phrase Technique' and 'Mental Snapshot Method' respectively. Use the colour green for all these five sub-branches.

Step 5—From the second branch, Linking, draw two branches and label them 'Pure Link Method' and 'Story Link Method' respectively. Use the colour green for these two subheadings.

Step 6—From the third branch, Pegging, draw two main branches for the 'Number Peg System' and the 'Alphabet Peg System'. Use the colour green for these subheadings. From the Number Peg System, draw three branches and label them 'The Number Shape System', 'The Number Rhyme System' and 'The Major System' respectively. From the Alphabet Peg System, draw two branches and label them 'Familiar Peg Words' and 'Alphabet Rhyme System' respectively. Use the colour purple for these sub-subheadings.

Step 7—From the fourth branch, Journeys, Nicknames and Mind Maps, draw three branches and label them 'Journeys', 'Nicknames' and 'Mind Maps' respectively. This is done in the colour red as these are still main headings. From the heading labelled 'Journeys', draw three branches in the colour green and label them 'The Route Journey Method', 'The Room Journey Method' and 'The Body Journey Method'.

Step 8—You can add information such as the uses of each technique. For example, for long lists, short lists, anniversaries, passwords, etc. Instead of writing down the words, perhaps you can use symbols or pictures to denote the subheadings as well. Make sure each heading and subheading is in a different colour. When you close your eyes, you should be able to see all the colours clearly and this will help you differentiate between the headings and subheadings. You can use the colour codes to differentiate headings and subheadings or even one chapter from another! This is completely up to you!

Exercise 2: Mind Map of Biology Project

Your teacher asks you to do a group project in biology about the major organs of the human body. Your group consisting of four members—Aishwarya, Thejas, Ayesha and you—decides to do the project on the brain, lungs, liver and heart. Each of you chooses one organ to work with. As the group leader, how do you coordinate between your teammates and oversee the project?

1. Deadline—when do you need to submit?
2. Time management.

3. Allot work to different teammates:
   a) Aishwarya—clay model of brain
   b) Thejas—chart of lungs
   c) Ayesha—verbal presentation of liver
   d) You—computer simulation of heart
4. Information—research from books, the Internet, journals, interacting with professionals.
5. Decide on what information to use.
6. Materials required (clay, chart paper, software, research material, tools, art supplies, etc.).
7. Internal resources—school laboratory, school computers, biology teacher.
8. External resources—speak to a cardiologist, buy software for simulation, take help from parents.
9. Team meetings—after school, during weekends.
10. How to present the work—who will present, how, etc.

Utilizing Memory Techniques

Every individual has his or her own unique way of learning, so try each of the memory techniques and discover which techniques suit you the best. For example, since you have the Number Rhyme System and the Number Shape System to translate numbers under 10 into images, you don't need to know both systems. Choose the system that you are most comfortable with and practise it.

You can mix and match the memory systems, as you will see in the following chapters. Again, choose the memory systems that you are most comfortable with and combine them. This will help you remember a combination of numbers and letters which will enable you to study historical dates, the periodic table, addresses, telephone numbers, etc. It is a matter of picking the techniques that you like and combining them in a way that fits your own thought process.

You can even make up your own systems using the principles of association, visualization, imagination and location that you have learnt in this book. Make it enjoyable and have fun. This way your brain will relax and you will learn new information quickly.

SUMMARY

Journeys

- Uses landmarks on locations to act as pegs to associate new information.

Route Journey Method

- Follows a fixed map. Certain landmarks are used as pegs along this route. To remember information, you need to associate each bit of information with each landmark. Now, simply walk through the route in your mind and you will be able to 'see' what you need to remember at each landmark.

Room Journey Method

- Similar to Route Journey Method but follows a specific path within your own home, using landmarks inside your house as pegs.

Body Journey Method

- Similar to Route Journey and Room Journey Methods but follows specific body parts starting from your head to your toes.

Nicknames

- Uses nicknames to associate related information such as capitals and currencies of countries, inventors and their inventions, etc.

- Once the nicknames are formed, the Story Link Method is used to associate the items.

Mind Maps

- Helps you understand information visually.
- Helps you consolidate large amounts of information by representing them on one page.

EXERCISE 1: MIND MAPS OF MEMORY TECHNIQUES

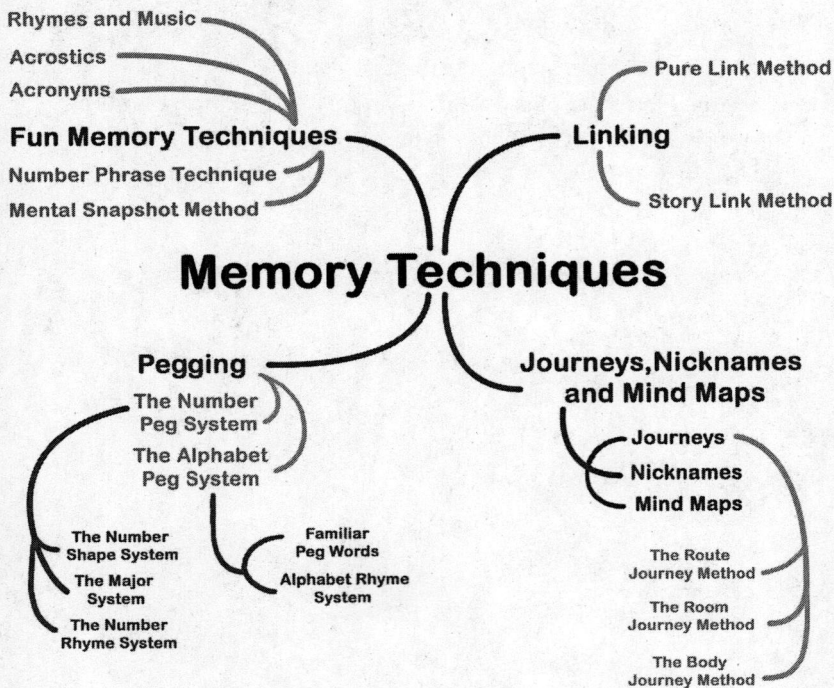

Rhymes and Music

Acrostics

Acronyms

Fun Memory Techniques

Number Phrase Technique

Mental Snapshot Method

Pure Link Method

Linking

Story Link Method

Memory Techniques

Pegging

The Number
Peg System

The Alphabet
Peg System

The Number
Shape System

The Major
System

The Number
Rhyme System

Familiar
Peg Words

Alphabet Rhyme
System

**Journeys, Nicknames
and Mind Maps**

Journeys

Nicknames

Mind Maps

The Route
Journey Method

The Room
Journey Method

The Body
Journey Method

Chapter 7

Applying Memory Techniques in Academics

Now that you have learnt all the memory techniques, you will need to apply them in academics and also in your daily life. Before proceeding, make sure that you are thorough with the memory techniques.

Learning a Second Language

Studies have shown that bilingual people have a higher IQ than people who speak just one language. When you learn a different language, you are forcing your brain to adapt to something completely different and therefore your brain will get stimulated more and your analytic and memory skills will improve.

Most people learn a second language or even a third language in school. The skills that you need to utilize while learning a new language include reading, writing, speaking, listening, understanding, memorizing and taking tests. Additional skills require learning gender-based words, grammatical rules, sentence structure, verb conjugations, prefixes, suffixes and basic roots of the language. For example, languages like Marathi, Bengali, Gujarati, Nepali, Punjabi and Hindi are all derived from the root language Sanskrit and, therefore, have similar words and sentence structures.

When you are just starting to learn a new language, memorization and repetition are the key. Since a new language is just a combination of sounds that initially hold no meaning, you need to give it some meaning so that you can understand it better. But simply translating from a second language to English may not be enough for this association to be strong. For example, the French word for dream is 'rêver' which does not sound like dream at all and has no memorable association to help you remember its meaning. However, if you give it a memorable association, you will be able to remember it better. Since the French word rêver sounds like the English word river, you can imagine a 'river of dreams' or 'dreaming about rivers'. This will help you remember both the French word and its meaning.

To learn a new language, you can use the Nickname Method. The key as always, is to use the memory building blocks of visualization, association, imagination and location to see the image clearly in your mind. Let's apply this system to a few words in French and Spanish to help with vocabulary.

Exercise 1: French to English Meanings

Work out the following using the Nickname Method. The first five are already worked out for you. Once you are done, read only the French words and see if you can remember their English meanings. If you need to remember the entire list of fifteen words, use the Pure Link System once you have finished learning the meanings.

	Meaning	Nickname	Association
French English	Chou (shoo) Cabbage	Shoe Cabbage	A cabbage rotting in your shoe!
French English	Glace (glas) Ice	Glass Ice	Your window made of ice instead of glass.
French English	Fromage Cheese	From age Cheese	The old cheese is stinking from age.

French	Craindre	Crane	I'm afraid of cranes!
English	To be afraid of	To be afraid of	
French	Bois (Bua)	Boa	The boa constrictor slithered
English	Wood	Wood	up the wood.
French	Début (day bue)		
English	Beginning		
French	Avocat		
English	Lawyer		
French	Salle		
English	Room		
French	Tout (toot)		
English	Everything		
French	Remercier (remers-e-air)		
English	To thank		
French	Lundi		
English	Monday		
French	Bateau (bat-oh)		
English	Boat/Ship		
French	Sauter (sot-ay)		
English	To jump		
French	Neuf (nerf)		
English	Nine		
French	Jambe		
English	Leg		

Exercise 2: Spanish to English Meanings

Here are a few common words in Spanish. The first five are worked out for you. Try and work out the rest.

	Meaning	Nickname	Association
Spanish	Seta	Set of	Would you like a set
English	Mushrooms	Mushrooms	of mushrooms?
Spanish	Venda	Vending machine	Let's buy bands from
English	Band	Band	a vending machine!
Spanish	Vasa	Vase	Drinking out of a
English	Glass	Glass	vase instead of a glass.
Spanish	Pluma	Plume	Writing on a plume
English	Pen	Pen	of feathers with a pen.
Spanish	Pajaro	Mitsubishi Pajero	A bird driving a
English	Bird	Bird	Mitsubishi Pajero
Spanish	Madre (madray)		
English	Mother		
Spanish	Cara		
English	Face		
Spanish	Mono		
English	Monkey		
Spanish	Perro		
English	Dog		
Spanish	Comida		
English	Lunch		
Spanish	El libro		
English	Book		
Spanish	Dibujar		
English	To draw		
Spanish	La playa		
English	Beach		
Spanish	El Mercado		
English	Market		
Spanish	Comprar		
English	To buy		

Exercise 3: Learning Difficult Words in English

Using the same technique that you used with foreign languages, you can break down difficult English words and then associate the broken down words to their meanings so that they become more memorable.

		Nickname	Association
English Meaning	Neophyte Beginner	Knee-fight Beginner	A beginner's level boxing match where the contestants are on their knees, fighting.
English Meaning	Adumbrate Give summary of	A-dumb-rate Summary	The summary of the entire lesson was given at a dumb rate.
English Meaning	Blandishment Flattery intended to persuade	Bland-dish-ment Flatter intended to persuade	He flattered the cook and persuaded him to make a bland dish meant for babies.
English Meaning	Callous Emotionally hardened	Call-us Emotionally hardened	Call us on our helpline if you're emotionally hardened!
English Meaning	Debunk Expose while ridiculing	The-bunk Expose while ridiculing	He fell off the bunk, exposing his ugly tattoo and was ridiculed for it.

English Meaning	Ebullient Joyfully unrestrained	E-bull-ient Joyfully unrestrained	
English Meaning	Forbearance Good-natured tolerance		
English Meaning	Grandiloquent Lofty in style		
English Meaning	Incontrovertible Impossible to disprove		
English Meaning	Mendacious Given to lying		

Pro Tips:

- Always convert new words to more understandable words and associated images. See the image clearly in your mind. The more you practice, the clearer your images will become.
- The more images you create, the greater capacity you will have to remember them and your memory will become stronger.
- By using visualization and imagination, create an association between the foreign word or the difficult word and its English meaning and turn it into a mental image.
- You can either substitute other words or use a similar sounding word to create your mental image.
- Use the first image that comes to mind as this will form a stronger association.
- Understand the roots of the language that you are studying—everything from grammar to sentence structure. Try to expose yourself to the language as much as possible by watching movies, reading books, and trying to converse where possible.

Memorizing Historic Events and Dates

History gives you a context to the reality that you live in at present. It describes the struggles that your ancestors went through so that you can enjoy the freedom that you have today and don't repeat the same mistakes that they made.

History is basically composed of a sequence of events, so you may need to remember the order of events to score better marks. It may help to create connections between each fact that you study so that one fact may link to the next fact. It may also help to divide each piece of information into a) causes of an event, b) details of the event and, c) outcome or consequences of the event. You can do this with the help of Mind Maps. Once you have done this, you can flesh it out with more information.

It is mandatory to know certain important dates in history such as the year that India got independence, when the Sepoy Movement took place, when the First and Second World Wars started, the formation of the UNO, etc. To remember historical events along with their dates, you can use a combination of memory techniques. You can use the Number Shape or the Number Rhyme method or the Major System to remember the days of the month. You can use certain peg words for the month along with the Major System to remember the year. You can then use the Story Link Method to associate the date with the event.

The following are a list of twelve peg words to denote each month based on some event that happens in that month or an important day that falls in that month. You can either use these peg words or make up your own peg words depending on the month on which your birthday falls or what each month means to you.

Month	Important Event/Day	Peg Word
January	Wintertime	Snowflakes
February	Valentine's Day	Hearts/Flowers
March	Exams	Question papers
April	April Fool's Day	Joker
May	Labour Day	Labourers working in a field
June	Father's Day	Father
July	Monsoon season	Umbrella
August	Independence Day	Flag
September	Teacher's Day	Teacher
October	Halloween	Pumpkin
November	Thanksgiving Day	Turkey
December	Christmas Day	Christmas Tree

Always convert dates to the day/month/year format so that you do not get mixed up between the American System of dates and the British System of dates. So, if you want to remember that Jawaharlal Nehru was born on 14 November 1889, you first need to write it as 14/Nov/1889 and then convert the numbers to words using any of the systems. Here, you can use the Major System to convert the number 14 to **tire**, the month of November is converted to a **turkey** and 1889 is converted to its letters of **nffb**. Since 1 is common to most dates in the last 1,000 years, you can disregard this and use only the letters for 889 which are **ffb**. The year is further converted into words using the Major System so you can convert 889 as **five** (88) **bee** (9) or **foe** (8) **vibe** (89) to denote the year 1889. Now you can use the Story Link Method to put all the words together including Jawaharlal Nehru.

Jawaharlal Nehru + tire + turkey +foe + vibe = **Jawaharlal**

Nehru tirelessly used a **turkey** to fight his **foes**, which gave India a positive **vibe**.

Let's try this with a few more historically significant dates.

1. 29 March 1857—Revolt by Mangal Pandey at Barrackpore
   If you've seen the movie, you can clearly picture Aamir Khan as Mangal Pandey in his red uniform. The date '29' can be converted to either a duck and badminton racket using the Number Shape Method or a **nib**, using the Major System. March is converted to question papers, 1857 can be converted to 857 or flk, which is then converted to a word—**flack** or **fluke**. So you have Mangal Pandey + Nib + Question Papers + Flack. Using the Story Link Method, associate these words—**Mangal Pandey** furiously writing with his **nib** on his **question papers** and getting **flack** for it or **Mangal Pandey** hitting a **duck** with his **badminton racket**. It hits some British soldiers who are answering **question papers**, which is a **fluke!**

2. 1 September 1939—Second World War started
   Using the Number Rhyme Method, 1 can be converted to bun, September is converted to teacher and 939 can be converted to bmp or **bump**. Second World War started when a teacher fired a bun with a bump!

3. 24 October 1945—United Nations Organization (UNO) was set up.
   Conversion—24—He**nr**y (Major System)
   —October—Pumpkin
   —945—brl—**Barrel**
   Story Link—UNO was started by Henry when he threw a pumpkin in a barrel!

4. 1905—Swadeshi Movement
   Conversion—905—pzl—puzzle
   Story Link—The Swadeshi movement was a **puzzle** to the Britishers.

5. 1942—Quit India Movement
   Conversion—942—brn—**Brain**
   Story Link—The Quit India Movement was started by using our brain!

6. 1920—Non-Cooperation Movement
   Conversion—920—bns—**Bounce**
   Story Link—Did the Non-Cooperation Movement **bounce** all over India?

7. 1919—Jallianwala Bagh Massacre
   Conversion—919—btb—**bee + tub**
   The Jallianwala Bagh massacre started with a bee bouncing off a tub.

8. 12 March 1930—The Dandi March
   Conversion—12—Shelf (Number Rhyme)
   —March—Question papers
   —930—bms—**Bombs**
   Story Link—The Dandi March happened on a shelf with question papers and no bombs!

9. 20 April 1889—Birth of Adolf Hitler
   Conversion—20—ns—Nose (Major System)
   —April—Joker
   —889—fvb—**five bee**
   Story Link—Adolf Hitler had a nose like a joker and got stung by five bees.

10. 26 January 1950—Dr Rajendra Prasad became the first

president of India.

Conversion—26—nudge (Major System)

—January—Snowflake

—950—pls—**Palace**

Story Link—Can Dr Rajendra Prasad nudge a snowflake in the palace?

Exercise 4: Timeline of Mahatma Gandhi's Life

Now that you have learnt this system of remembering dates and years in history, apply it to the timeline of Mahatma Gandhi's life. You can use the Nickname Method to associate the dates with the events.

1. 2 October 1869—Gandhi was born in Porbandar
    Conversions—2 _____
    —October _____
    —869 _____
    —Porbandar—Pour+Band+Are _____
    Story Link _____

2. 1882—Gandhi was married to Kasturba
    Conversions—882 _____
    —Kasturba _____
    Story Link _____

3. 1887—Went to England for higher studies
    Conversions _____
    —Higher Studies _____
    Story Link _____

4. 1890—Returned to India with a law degree
    Conversions—890 _____
    —Law degree _____
    Story Link _____

5. 1892—Went to South Africa
   Conversions—892 _____
   —South Africa _____
   Story Link _____

6. 1894—Organized Natal Indian Congress
   Conversions—894 _____
   —NIC _____
   Story Link _____

7. 1909—Organized Satyagraha in South Africa
   Conversions—909 _____
   —Satyagraha _____
   Story Link _____

8. 1915—Returned to India
   Conversions—915 _____
   —India _____
   Story Link _____

9. 1916—Set up Ashram at Sabarmati
   Conversions—916 _____
   —Ashram _____
   —Sabarmati _____
   Story Link _____

10. 1917—Satyagraha at Champaran
    Conversions—917 _____
    —Satyagraha _____
    —Champaran _____
    Story Link _____

11. 1920—Non-Cooperation Movement
    Conversions—920 _____
    Non-Cooperation Movement _____

Story Link _____

12. 1924—Elected president of the Indian National Congress
    Conversions—924 _____
    President of INC _____
    Story Link _____

13. 12 March, 1930—Dandi March
    Conversions—12 _____
    —March _____
    —930 _____
    Dandi March _____
    Story Link _____

14. 1931—Gandhi–Irwin Pact
    Conversions—931 _____
    Gandhi-Irwin Pact _____
    Story Link _____

15. 1936—Set up Sewagram at Wardha
    Conversions—936 _____
    Sewagram at Wardha _____
    Story Link _____

16. 1942—Quit India Movement launched
    Conversions—942 _____
    Quit India Movement _____
    Story Link _____

17. 1946—Went on pilgrimage to Noakhali
    Conversions—946 _____
    Pilgrimage _____
    Noakhali _____
    Story Link _____

18. 30 January 1948—Assassinated

Conversions—30 _____

—January _____

—948 _____

Assassinated _____

Story Link _____

Pro Tips:

- If all the events that you have studied are in the same century, then you can disregard the first two digits of the year and concentrate on converting only the last two digits into a word or an image. For example, India's freedom struggle occurred between 1857 and 1947. If you remember the events that happened in the 1800s, you can disregard '18' and convert only the last two digits of the year.

- If you are memorizing events that happened in different centuries, you can colour code centuries so that you do not have to convert the first two numbers of the year. For example, events that happened in the 15th century can be assigned the colour red, events that happened in the 16th century can be assigned blue, events of the 17th century can be assigned yellow, etc. Now when you visualize these events, just picture them with an overtone of the corresponding colour. This will save you the trouble of converting the 15 in 1598 into words or images.

- You can use any of the Number Systems to remember the dates, as long as you remember which system you used when converting the story links back to numbers. To be on the safer side, always use the Number Shape or Number Rhyme system for the days and the Major System for the years or the Major System for days as well as years. Use the same Peg words for months.

- You can remember the entire list by using the Journey Method and placing each point or key word at one location. For example, to remember Gandhiji's life events, you can place his date of birth at your front door (first landmark), his marriage to Kasturba at the front gate (second landmark), his higher studies in England under a tree (third landmark), etc. In this way, while you walk through your familiar route in your mind, you will remember his life events in the correct order.

Learning the Periodic Table

You have already studied the first twenty elements of the periodic table under the acrostic section. You can continue using acrostics for the entire periodic table by learning all the elements in their respective groups.

Group 1—The alkali metals—(H, Li, Na, K, Rb, Cs, Fr)
Highly Nasty Kids Rub Cats Fur
H—Hydrogen, **Li**—Lithium, **Na**—Sodium, **K**—Potassium, **Rb**—Rubidium, **Cs**—Caesium, **Fr**—Francium

Group 2—The alkaline earth metals—(Be, Mg, Ca, Sr, Ba, Ra)
Beer Mugs Can Serve Bar Rats
Be—Beryllium, **Mg**—Magnesium, **Ca**—Calcium, **Sr**—Strontium, **Ba**—Barium, **Ra**—Radium

Group 13—The boron family—(B, Al, Ga, In, Tl)
Bears Always Gave Indians Trouble.
B—Boron, **Al**—Aluminium, **Ga**—Gallium, **In**—Indium, **Tl**—Thallium

Group 14—The carbon family—(C, Si, Ge, Sn, Pb)
Can Silly Germs Snatch Lead?
C—Carbon, **Si**—Silicon, **Ge**—Germanium, **Sn**—Tin, **Pb**—Lead

Group 15—Nitrogen Family—(N, P, As, Sb, Bi)
Never Put Arsenic (in) **Sibling's Beer.**
N—Nitrogen, **P**—Phosphorus, **As**—Arsenic, **Sb**—Antimony,
Bi—Bismuth

Group 16—Oxygen Family—The Chalcogens—(O, S, Se, Te, Po)
Old Surf Seems Terribly Polluted.
O—Oxygen, **S**—Sulfur, **Se**—Selenium, **Te**—Tellurium, **Po**—
Polonium

Group 17—Fluorine family—The Halogens—(F, Cl, Br, I, At)
'**Floor Cleaner Broken?' I A**sked.
F—Fluorine, **Cl**—Chlorine, **Br**—Bromine, **I**—Iodine, **At**—
Astatine

Group 18—Helium family—Noble Gases—(He, Ne, Ar, Kr, Xe, Rn)
He Needs OUR Crazy Xerox Repairman.
He—Helium, **Ne**—Neon, **Ar**—Argon, **Kr**—Krypton, **Xe**—Xenon,
Rn—Radon

First Row Transition Metals—(Sc, Ti, V, Cr, Mn, Fe, Co, Ni, Cu, Zn)
Scott Tickled Vanna's Cranium, Manager Fed Cold Nuggets (to)
Cute Zebras.
Sc—Scandium, **Ti**—Titanium, **V**—Vanadium, **Cr**—Chromium,
Mn—Manganese, **Fe**—Iron, **Co**—Cobalt, **Ni**—Nickel, **Cu**—
Copper, **Zn**—Zinc

Second Row Transition Metals—(Y, Zr, Nb, Mo, Tc, Ru, Rh, Pd, Ag, Cd)
Yes, Zephyr Nob Most Technicians Rub Rod's Pale Silver
Cadillac.
Y—Yttrium, **Zr**—Zirconium, **Nb**—Niobium, **Mo**—Molybdenum,

Tc—Technetium, **Ru**—**Ru**thenium, **Rh**—**Rh**odium, **Pd**—Palladium, **Ag**—Silver, **Cd**—Cadmium

Third Row Transition Metals—(La, Hf, Ta, W, Re, Os, Ir, Pt, Au, Hg)
Larry **H**alf **Ta**med **W**endy **Re**sulting (in) **Os**sy **Ir**rationally **P**leading (for) **Au**drey's **Hug**.
L—Lanthanum, **Hf**—**Hf**afnium, **Ta**—**Ta**ntalum, **W**—Tungsten, **Re**—**Re**hnium, **Os**—**Os**mium, **Ir**—**Ir**idium, **Pt**—Platinum, **Au**—Gold, **Hg**—Mercury.

Lanthanides—(Ce, Pr, Nd, Pm, Sm, Eu, Gd, Tb, Dy, Ho, Er, Tm, Yb, Lu)
Caesar **Pr**ocrastinated **N**eeding **P**ermission(from) **S**ome **Eu**ropeans (who were) **G**ood (in) **T**ubs **D**yed **Ho**ney, **Er**ring **T**hem(to) **Y**ell '**Lutetium**!'
Ce—**Ce**rium, **Pr**—**Pr**aseodymium, **Nd**—**N**eodymium, **Pm**—**P**romethium, **Sm**—**S**amarium, **Eu**—**Eu**ropium, **Gd**—**G**adolinium, **Tb**—**T**erbium, **Dy**—**Dy**sprosium, **Ho**—**Ho**lmium, **Er**—**Er**bium, **Tm**—**T**hulium, **Yb**—**Y**tterbium, **Lu**—**Lu**tetium.

Actinides—(Th, Pa, U, Np, Pu, Am, Cm, Bk, Cf, Es, Fm, Md, No, Lr)
Three **Pl**anets: **U**ranus, **N**eptune, (and) **Pl**uto **A**im (to) **C**ome (to)**B**erkeley, **C**alifornia. **E**instein (and) **F**ermi **M**ade **N**oble **L**aws.
Th—**Th**orium, **Pa**—**P**rotactinium, **U**—**U**ranium, **Np**—**N**eptunium, **Pu**—**P**lutonium, **Am**—**Am**ericium, **Cm**—**C**urium, **Bk**—**B**erkelium, **Cf**—**C**alifornium, **Es**—**E**insteinium, **Fm**—**F**ermium, **Md**—**M**endelevium, **No**—**No**bleium, **Lr**—**L**awrencium.

Now that you have learnt all the elements in the periodic table, let's see how you can remember each group. If you were to go to a party and you saw a guest list, perhaps one or two names might stand out but the list itself would be meaningless to you.

As the evening progresses and you begin to talk and interact with other guests, you might be able to remember their names better. After the party, you might be able to remember that the girl in the green dress was Jenny and you were talking to her in the dining room, or that the football player was Jeff and you were talking to him in the garden. You will also be able to remember certain groups that had formed and who was talking to whom.

In the same way, just learning the list of elements may not be enough to cement them in your memory but once you place them in groups in certain locations, they may be easier to recall. By designating specific locations for specific groups of the elements, you can avoid confusing them and mixing them up with other groups. For this, you can use the Journey Method.

Imagine a building that has thirteen rooms, one room for each group of elements discussed above. Maybe you can picture your school campus with its auditorium, library, labs, field, basketball court, etc. Now, let's take a guided tour around your school.

At the first stop, you have the school auditorium, where you will place the Group 1 elements. You can perhaps picture a candle burning at the auditorium door to signify the number 1 (Number Shape System) for Group 1.

Your next stop or landmark is your biology laboratory where you will place all the Group 2 elements. There is a duck (Number Shape for 2) standing guard at the door.

Your next stop is the cafeteria, where you will place all the Group 13 elements of the Boron family. The cafeteria is decorated with candles and giant hearts (Number shape for 13).

Stop number 4 is the basketball court, where you will place all the Group 14 elements of the carbon family. The basketball court is filled with lit candles on sailboats (Number Shape for 14).

Stop number 5 is the library, where you will place the Group 15 elements of the nitrogen family. The door handle of the library is shaped like a seahorse and since there is no electricity, the library is lit with candles (Number Shape for 15).

Continue in the same way for the rest of the groups.

Location 6—Group 16—Location and Number Shape _____

_____

Location 7—Group 17—Location and Number Shape _____

_____

Location 8—Group 18—Location and Number Shape _____

_____

Location 9—First row transition metals—Location and Image for 'first row' _____

_____

Location 10—Second row transition metals—Location and Image for 'second row' _____

_____

Location 11—Third row transition metals—Location and Image for 'third row' _____

_____

Location 12—Lanthanides—Location and Nickname for 'Lanthanides' _____

_____

Location 13—Actinides—Location and Nickname for 'Actinides'

_____

_____

The above exercise is important to visualize because the following exercise is connected to this and you will be revisiting these locations after completing the next exercise. So far, you have studied the list of elements in the periodic table according to their groups and you have placed each group in a particular location in your school. Next, you are going to learn the atomic number for each element. For this, you need to combine the technique that you learnt to study foreign languages and history dates, which is essentially combining the Nickname Method and the Major System of numbers.

Rather than go according to the atomic number of each element, you will continue to work with the above elements in their groups. Using the building blocks of visualization, imagination and association, picture each element with its atomic number in each location.

Start with **Group 1, which is in the auditorium of your school, with a candle at the front door.**

Element	Element Image	Atomic Number	Major System
Hydrogen (H)	Hydrogen balloon	1	Tie

Story Link—Hydrogen balloon dressed in formals, wearing a tie.

Lithium (Li)	Litchi	3	Ma

Story Link—Ma eating litchis.

Sodium (Na)	Soda	11	Tot

Story Link—Tiny tot drinking soda.

Potassium (K)	Pot stash	19	Tub

Story Link—Pot stashed in a tub.

| Rubidium (Rb) | Rub | 37 | Mickey |

Story Link—Mickey Mouse rubbing his injured knee.

| Caesium (Cs) | Caesar | 55 | Lolly |

Story Link—Julius Caesar is eating an ice lolly.

| Francium (Fr) | France | 87 | Fish |

Story Link—It's raining fish in France!

Story Link for Group 1—Picture yourself entering your school auditorium that has a candle burning at the door. As soon as you enter, you see a hydrogen balloon, dressed up formally wearing a tie. As you go further in, you see your Ma eating litchis. Next to her is a tiny tot drinking soda, standing next to a pot stashed in a tub. As you move further inside, you see Mickey Mouse rubbing his injured knee while Julius Caesar is eating his ice lolly. Suddenly, it starts raining fish and you realize you're in France!

Group 2—Biology laboratory with a duck standing guard at the entrance.

Element	Element image	Atomic Number	Major System Image
Beryllium (Be)	Berry	4	Row

Story Link—Rows and rows of berries.

| Magnesium (Mg) | Magazines | 12 | Den |

Story Link—Aden piled high with magazines.

| Calcium (Ca) | Calcium Tablets | 20 | Nose |

Story Link—Shoving calcium tablets up your nose.

| Strontium (Sr) | Straw | 38 | Movie |

Story Link—A movie about straws.

| Barium (Ba) | Barry | 56 | Leash |

Story Link—Barry on a leash!

| Radium (Ra) | Radius | 88 | Five |

Story Link—The radius of that table is five!

Story Link for Group 2—You leave the auditorium and move on to the biology laboratory that has a duck standing guard at the entrance. As soon as you enter, you see rows and rows of berries. Once you have waded through all the berries, you come to a den piled high with magazines. Since the magazines are dusty and make you sneeze, you shove some calcium tablets up your nose and then decide to watch a movie about straws. In the movie, you see your friend Barry on a leash jumping up and down on a round table. He stares at you and says, 'The radius of this table is five, of course!'

Work out the element image and story link for the following groups. When you have finished with one group, write down the story link for the whole group. The images for the Major System are taken from the list in chapter 5, but feel free to put in your own images.

Group 13—The Cafeteria, decorated with candles and giant hearts.

Element	Element Image	Atomic Number	Major System Image
Boron (B)	5	Law	

Story Link _____

Aluminium (Al) 13	Tin

Story Link _____

Gallium (Ga) 31	Mat

Story Link _____

Indium (In) 49	Robe

Story Link _____

Thallium (Tl) 81	Feet

Story Link _____

Story Link for Group 13 _____

_____

_____

_____

_____

Group 14—Basketball court with lit candles on sailboats on it.

Element	Element Image	Atomic Number	Major System Image
Carbon (C)	6	Jaw	

Story Link _____

Silicon (Si)	14	Tire	

Story Link _____

Germanium	32	Man	

Story Link _____

Tin (Sn)	50	Lace	

Story Link _____

Lead (Pb)	82	Fan	

Story Link _____

Story Link for Group 14 _____

_____

_____

_____

_____

Group 15—The library lit with candles and the door handle shaped like a seahorse.

Element	Element Image	Atomic Number	Major System Image
Nitrogen (N)	7	Cow	
Story Link	_____		
Phosphorus (P)	15	Toll (booth)	
Story Link	_____		
Arsenic (As)	33	Mom	
Story Link	_____		
Antimony (Sb)	51	Loot	
Story Link	_____		
Bismuth (Bi)	83	Fame	
Story Link	_____		

Story Link for Group 15 _____

_____

_____

_____

_____

Exercise 5

Take a paper or a notebook and write down the rest of the groups in the same way as listed above. Once you are done, mentally walk through your school starting from the auditorium and moving through the biology laboratory, etc. and try to see these elements at these locations. While you are doing so, you can repeat the acrostic for each group in your mind so that you know the order of elements once you enter the appropriate location. Observing what these elements are doing (story link) will tell you their atomic numbers.

Pro Tips:

- While it has taken a few pages to describe this technique, remember that it takes only a few seconds to follow the instructions so do not despair about the length. Once you are proficient with the memory systems, following the steps mentioned above will be a piece of cake.
- While doing the acrostics for the groups, be careful of elements that start with the same letter. For this the context of the elements comes into play. For example, if you are getting confused between barium and boron, you should know that since barium is an alkaline earth metal, it is in Group 2 and since boron is in the boron family, it is in Group 13.
- Use acrostics to learn the elements in their groups. Assign each group to a different location in your school, using the Journey Method. Once this is done, use the Nickname method and Major Systems to link each element to their respective atomic numbers.
- Once you have finished the entire exercise from beginning to end, make sure you revise it so that it stays in your long-term memory.

Learning Poems, Monologues and Speeches

Ancient Romans and Greeks were good at memorizing and making long speeches. In fact, they took pride in their amazing memory to recall long texts. With little or no writing material available at the time, it was common for orators and poets to memorize their material by imagining a journey and placing each item that was to be remembered at a certain landmark. You can use the Journey Method as well to memorize poems, monologues and speeches.

Poems

When memorizing poems, it helps to first read the poem and see how much you can remember without memory aids. Try to grasp the meaning of the poem, notice the syntax, rhyming words, and literary tools that the poet has used. For example, if it is a sonnet, you know that it will have fourteen lines in a particular rhythm. Study and read everything that you have been taught in class. This will give you a good context and a better understanding of the poem.

Let's look at the poem, 'The Road Not Taken' by Robert Frost. It has twenty lines and so you will have to plan a route that has twenty stops or landmarks. You can either do this in your house with landmarks in each room or outdoors with the route that you take to school. You can even do it in your school building, as you did with the periodic table, and choose landmarks within the buildings. For this example, you can use an outdoor route from your front door to your classroom and fix twenty landmarks along the way. You can then peg each landmark to each line of the poem as follows:

'The Road Not Taken'
by Robert Frost

Front door of your house	Two roads diverged in a yellow wood,
Front gate	And sorry I could not travel both
Tree	And be one traveler, long I stood

Beauty Parlour	And looked down one as far as I could
Traffic light	To where it bent in the undergrowth;
Bakery	Then took the other, as just as fair,
Petrol bunk	And having perhaps the better claim,
Bus stop	Because it was grassy and wanted wear;
Restaurant	Though as for that the passing there
Bookstore	Had worn them really about the same,
Supermarket	And both that morning equally lay
Movie theatre	In leaves no step had trodden black.
Park	Oh, I kept the first for another day!
Lake	Yet knowing how way leads on to way,
Field	I doubted if I should ever come back.
Shopping mall	I shall be telling this with a sigh
Metro Station	Somewhere ages and ages hence:
Pub	Two roads diverged in a wood, and I—
School front gate	I took the one less traveled by,
Classroom	And that has made all the difference.

Step 1—Understand the context of the poem. Robert Frost was a farmer in America but he moved to England and was contemplating whether to take up writing or to continue farming. He was at a crossroad in his life and the decision that he was about to take would make all the difference.

Step 2—Write down the landmarks and the line to be pegged to each side by side as above.

Step 3—Identify certain keywords in each line.

Step 4—At every landmark, make an association between the landmark and the first word of the poem in addition to the key word that you have chosen. In some lines, the keywords may just be concepts and nothing concrete. In these instances, you will need to convert the concept into a more concrete word or image. For example, the line 'Though as for that the passing there' does not have a concrete image and therefore you will need to convert one of the words into a concrete image or word. The word 'passing' seems to be the keyword in that phrase. You can convert this into a concrete image by picturing Gandalf's famous line in *The Lord of the Rings* where he yells 'You shall not pass!' at the orcs. Another image associated with 'passing' is that of exams so you can picture yourself jumping for joy when you see that you have passed. In the context of the poem, 'passing' refers to people who have walked that path before so you can also picture ancient Neanderthals trudging the same path as Robert Frost.

Step 5—If you cannot find a particular key word, use the essence of the phrase itself for an image.

Now go line by line, associating the location to the first word of each line along with the key words. Try and get the essence of the lines as well when you make your associations.

Front door of your house + two + yellow wood
Association—You can't believe it! All of a sudden, your house has two front doors and the wood has turned yellow!

Front gate + and + Image of man looking sad
Association—At the front gate, you see **And**y looking sadly at the crossroads.

Tree + and + One traveller
Association—**And**y has now moved to the tree and you see him standing there for a long time with his suitcase.

Beauty parlour + and + Looked
Association—Andy has lugged his suitcase all the way to the beauty parlour where he is peering intently down the road.

Traffic light + to + Bent bushes (undergrowth)
Association—At the traffic light, he can see a duck (number shape for to/two) under some bushes that are bent and crooked.

Bakery + then + Took the other
Association—He picks up a hen (Then rhymes with ten, number rhyme for ten is hen) and walks in the other direction.

Petrol Bunk + and + Better Claim
Association—Once he reaches the petrol bunk, Andy butters a clam (sounds like better claim).

Bus stop + because + Grassy
Association—At the bus stop, he sees a bee causing a traffic jam on the grass.

Restaurant + though + Passing (Hint: though sounds like Toe)
Association _____

Bookstore + had + Same
Association _____

Supermarket + and + Morning
Association _____

Movie theatre + in + Trodden black
Association _____

Park + Oh + First (Hint: Oh [o] looks like a hula hoop)

Association _____

Lake + yet + Leads
Association _____

Field + I + come back
Association _____

Shopping mall + I + Sigh
Association _____

Metro station + Somewhere + Ages and ages
Association _____

Pub + Two + Wood
Association _____

School front gate + I + Less travelled
Association _____

Classroom + and + Difference
Association _____

Step 6—Now that you have completed the exercise, visualize your journey from your front door to your classroom with all twenty landmarks and see if you can remember the lines.

Memorizing Speeches and Monologues

The same method is followed to memorize speeches and monologues. First read through and study your speech or monologue and see how much you can remember. Then identify a keyword in each line. Plan your journey and associate each keyword to each landmark. When you are actually giving your speech, mentally walk from one landmark to the next, picturing each keyword at each landmark and you will be able to remember your speech in the correct sequence.

Pro Tips:

- Always use familiar locations as the landmarks of these locations are already in your long-term memory.
- You may either use the Route Journey Method or Room Journey method for long poems and speeches. The Body Journey Method can be used for shorter poems and speeches.
- If the speech or monologue is very long, keep adding landmarks to your route. You can add as many landmarks as you like to associate each sentence or phrase of the speech or monologue.
- If you would like to remember your speech in paragraphs, use the Room Journey Method with one room corresponding with one paragraph. Objects in that room can be used as landmarks for every sentence or phrase.

Learning English Spellings

Words That Sound the Same But Are Spelt Differently (Homophones)

In most cases, you may know the spellings of words but may get confused about which word to use if two or more words sound the same but are spelt differently. For example, piece and peace, to and too, lose and loose, etc. In this case, if you learn simple memory techniques to learn one word, by the process of elimination, you would automatically know that the other word is spelt differently.

Three memory techniques can be utilized to remember the different spellings of these words. The first technique is the Nickname Method, the second technique is simple associations, and the third technique is using the words in context to understand the difference in meaning of the words. This is done by making sentences with the words, and using them in the right context.

Example for Nickname Method: Male and Mail—The m**al**e's middle name was **Al**.

Example for simple associations: Stationery and Stationary—station**e**ry refers to writing or office materials, while station**a**ry refers to something that is not moving. If you associate the 'e' in stationery to 'envelope', you will always remember that station**e**ry refers to office materials while the word spelt with an 'a' refers to something that is not moving.

Example for context: Your and You're—**You are** (you're) intelligent, which means that **your** IQ is high.

Let's try these techniques with a few more words. Remember, by the process of elimination, once you know how to spell one word, you can remember the spelling for the other similar sounding word.

1. Piece and Peace—**Pie**ce of **pie**! By the process of elimination, you know that the other peace is the opposite of war.
2. Principal and Principle—My school princi**pal** is my **pal**.
3. Quiet and Quite—Please keep **quite** qui**e**t about my d**iet**.
4. Stair and Stare—Climb a st**air** into the **air**.
5. Throne and Thrown—**One** person can sit on a thr**one**.
6. Meat and Meet—**Eat** some m**eat**.
7. Witch and Which—The w**itch** had an **itch**. **Which witch?** That **witch!**
8. Hear and Here—You h**ear** with your **ear**.
9. Whose and Who's—W**hose hose** can I use to water the plants?
10. To and Too—**Too** many **o**'s.
11. Ball and Bawl _____
12. There and Their _____
13. Hole and Whole _____
14. Pear and Pair _____
15. Knows and Nose _____

16. Guessed and Guest _____
17. Beech (tree) and Beach _____
18. Plane and Plain _____
19. Through and Threw _____
20. Leak and Leek _____
21. Rain and Reign _____
22. Whine and Wine _____
23. Altar and Alter _____
24. Would and Wood _____
25. Heir and Air _____

Pro Tips:

• When learning words that sound the same but are spelled differently, use simple memory techniques to learn one word. Then, by the process of elimination, you automatically know that the other similar sounding word is spelled differently.

Words That Are Spelled the Same But Pronounced Differently (Heteronyms)

There are a few words that are spelt the same but differ in meaning, pronunciation and derivation. Usually one pronunciation is a verb while the other is a noun. For example, she wound (verb) the bandage around the wound (noun). As with the previous section, use context to differentiate the meaning of one word from the other. It helps to understand the meaning of the words before you make sentences with them.

Given below are a list of words that are spelt the same (mostly) but have different pronunciations and meanings. The first ten are worked out for you. Try to make sentences with the rest of the words based on their meanings. Verbs, nouns and adjectives are denoted by V, N and Adj respectively.

Heteronym	Pronunciation	Meaning	Used in Context
Produce	Prod-use	V: Manufacture	The farm was used to **produce** **produce**.
Produce	Pro-deuse	N: Agricultural Product	
Refuse	Ref-use	V: Say no to	The dump was so full, it had to **refuse** more **refuse**.
Refuse	Ref-use	N: Rubbish	
Polish	Paw-lish	V: Make shiny by running	We must **polish** the **Polish** furniture.
Polish	Pole-ish	Adj: Related to Poland	
Lead	Leed	V: Going in front of	He could **lead** if he could get the **lead** out.
Lead	Led	N: Metal	
Desert	Diz-ert	V: Abandon	The soldier decided to **desert** his **desert** in the **desert**.
Dessert	Diz-ert	V: Sweet	
Desert	Dez-ert	N: Land covered with sand	
Present	Prez-ent	N: Now	Since there was no time like the **present**, he thought he would **present** the **present** immediately.
Present	Priz-ent	V: Give someone	
Present	Prez-ent	N: Gift	
Bass	Bahs	N: Type of freshwater fish	A **bass** was painted on the **bass** drum.
Bass	Base	N: Lowest musical pitch	
Dove	Duv	N: Bird	When shot at, the **dove dove** into the bushes.
Dove	D-oh-v	V: Past tense of dive	

Object	Ob-ject	V: Express opposing view	I did not **object** to the **object**.
Object	Ob-ject	N: A thing	
Row	R-ow (ou)	N: Fight	There was a **row** amongst the **rows** of boatmen to teach how to **row** the boat.
Row	R-oh	N: Arranged in straight line	
Row	R-oh	V: Propel boat with oars	
Invalid	In-valid	Adj: Not valid	
Invalid	Invalid	N: Person disabled by illness	
Close	Cl-ose	Adj: Short distance away	
Close	Cl-oze	V: Cover an opening	
Does	Duz	V: Present tense of do	
Does	D-oh-s	N: Plural of doe, female deer	
Sewer	Soo-er	N: Underground drain	
Sewer	Soo-er	N: Person who sews	
Sow	S-ow	N: Adult female pig	
Sow	S-oh	V: To plant	
Wind	W-in-d	N: Rush of air	
Wind	Wine-d	V: Repeatedly twist or coil	
Minute	Minnit	N: 60 seconds	
Minute	Mine-yoot	Adj: Tiny	

Tear	Tare	V: Pull something apart	
Tear	T-year	N: Drops of liquid from eyes	
Bark	Bahk	N: Sharp explosive cry of dogs	
Bark	Bahk	N: Wood of the tree	
Intimate	Intimet	Adj: Closely acquainted with	
Intimate	Inti-mate	V: State or make known	

Pro Tip:

• When learning words that are spelt similarly but have a different meaning, first learn the meanings of the words and then form a sentence, using them in the correct context.

Commonly Misspelled Words

There are certain words in common vocabulary that are confusing and are almost always spelled wrong. For example, is it definitely or definately? Is it disappear or dissapear? Professor or professer? The Nickname Method and simple associations can be used to spell the correct word. Here are a few. The first ten are worked out for you. Try to find simple associations or nicknames for the next ten.

1. Cemetery or cemetary?—Three Es are buried in the c**e**m**e**t**e**ry.
2. Separate or seperate?—There's **a rat** in sep**arat**e!
3. Believe or beleive?—Never be**lie**ve a **lie**.
4. Argument or arguement? **Argue** lost an **E** in an **argu**ment!

5. Calendar or calender?—**Dar**a checked her calen**dar** every day.
6. Embarrass or embarass?—It's really hard to emba**rrass** **r**eally **r**ighteous and **s**erious students.
7. Exaggerate or exagerate?—**G**oofy **G**reg liked to exa**gg**erate.
8. Necessary or neccessary?—It is ne**cess**ary to remember the **cess** pool in the middle of the road.
9. Receive or recieve?—It's better to **gi**ve than to rece**i**ve.
10. Immediately or immedietely?—Mom **ate** immedi**ate**ly.
11. Definitely or definately? _____
12. Disappear or dissapear? _____
13. Professor or professor or professer? _____
14. Dilemma or dilemna? _____
15. Pavilion or pavillion? _____
16. Appearance or appearence? _____
17. Beginning or begining? _____
18. Committee or commitee? _____
19. Curiosity or curiousity? _____
20. Forty or fourty? _____

Pro Tip:

- When learning difficult spellings, use the Nickname Method and simple associations to spell the correct word.

Tricky words—Singular and Plural

English is a tricky language with grammatical rules that are not always followed. This makes it tough for non-English speakers and English speakers alike to learn spellings for the language since a grammar rule for one word may not apply to other words. For example,

> *I before E except when your foreign neighbour Keith receives eight counterfeit beige sleighs from feisty caffeinated weightlifters. Weird!*

the 'i before e except after c' rule applies to words such as ceiling, conceit, deceive, perceive, receipt, etc. but not to words such as ancient, concierge, glacier, science, efficient, etc.

Plurals are even more confusing. For example, the plural of mouse is mice but the plural of blouse is blouses. For the most part, plurals follow the grammar rule of add an 's' or 'es' or 'ies' or 'ves' after a singular to make it plural, but there are quite a few irregular verbs such as 'ox, man, woman, child, mouse, tooth, goose, foot' that do not follow these rules, as portrayed by the poem below. Learning this poem is more than enough to remember the irregular verbs and their plurals.

'Why English is So Hard'
By Anonymous

We'll begin with a box, and the plural is boxes,
But the plural of ox becomes oxen, not oxes.
One fowl is a goose, but two are called geese,
Yet the plural of moose should never be meese.
You may find a lone mouse or a nest full of mice,
Yet the plural of house is houses, not hice.

If the plural of man is always called men,
Why shouldn't the plural of pan be called pen?
If I speak of my foot and show you my feet,
And I give you a boot, would a pair be called beet?
If one is a tooth and a whole set are teeth,
Why shouldn't the plural of booth be called beeth?

Then one may be that, and three would be those,
Yet hat in the plural would never be hose,
And the plural of cat is cats, not cose.
We speak of a brother and also of brethren,

But though we say mother, we never say methren.
Then the masculine pronouns are he, his and him,
But imagine the feminine: she, shis and shim!

Pro Tip:

- It helps to know the irregular verbs so that you know that these verbs do not follow normal grammatical rules.

Effective Reading

Most of us study by reading our notes or studying from our textbooks. Some of you may read the same sentence over and over again to remember it better while others may take a long time to mull over each sentence before moving on to the next. However, your memory does not depend on the length of time it takes to read the study material, nor does it depend on mindless repetition. Often, while writing an exam, you may forget something that you thought you were thorough with. This is because you may have read the same thing a hundred times but you have not moved the study material from short-term memory to long-term memory.

There are a few techniques to help you read your study material more effectively. Although slightly unconventional, these techniques will help you focus, concentrate and understand your study material better.

1. You can make your reading and learning more effective by speeding up your reading. Speeding up reading actually helps you concentrate better and in turn, helps you understand the material better.

2. The next step to effective reading is to tell yourself that you are going to read the material only once in order to absorb the content. Avoid back-tracking and re-reading the sentences over and over again. This will help you focus completely on

what you are studying. If you read your study material with the attitude that you will be reading it again anyway, you are telling your mind that it doesn't have to focus so much the first time since it will have a second or third chance at the same material. As you can see, this will prove to be a waste of time.

3. In case you find the material difficult to understand, make note of it but don't stop reading. You can always ask a friend or refer to other sources of information for clarification later but continue reading at a steady pace. If you maintain steady eye movement over your notes, your comprehension will improve.

4. Use your finger as a guide to glide over words. Yes, you've been taught that using your fingers to point at words when you read is bad for you or bad manners and may inhibit or distract you from actual studying, but it actually aids you.

Here's an exercise to illustrate this. While keeping your head stationary, try scanning the room slowly from left to right with your eyes. If you notice, your eye movement would not have been smooth. Your eyes might have stopped at every object and then continued on. Now, repeat the exercise but this time, point your finger and move your hand from left to right slowly. Let your eyes focus on the end of your finger as it moves. You will notice that your eye movement was much smoother this time, even though the objects in the background might have been slightly blurred.

The same thing happens when you read. Your eyes stop for a fraction of a second at each word as you read sentences. The point at which your eyes stop is the point at which the information gets absorbed into your brain. Therefore, if your eye movement is smoother and you stop at the end of each sentence or even after each paragraph, you will absorb larger pieces of information and reduce the strain on your eyes. To do this, you need to use your finger to guide your eyes over words and sentences.

Developing a steady hand movement and rhythm is the key. Your brain will quickly accept that this new uninterrupted method of taking in information means that there is no time to stop or back-track over your notes. You can either use your finger or any other pointer such as a pen or pencil.

Exercise 6: Exercise in Effective Reading

Rest your finger just below a line and start moving it from left to right until your eyes are able to follow the text without pausing. Slowly increase the speed of your finger until the words become a blur. Don't worry too much about comprehension of the material at this point. Once you have found the upper limit, reduce the speed of your finger to a speed that is more comfortable for you. Chances are that this new comfortable speed is still much faster than your original reading speed.

Pro Tips:

- Have a mindset to read your syllabus only once while studying.
- Use your finger to point to the words as you read them to speed up your reading and encoding process.

Effective Note-Taking

Notes are vital in your studies as they help consolidate long lessons and help you focus on the key points and what is taught verbally in class. Taking notes is essential as they provide a good overview of a topic and give you a quick reference for exam revision. Since they are your own unique interpretation of the lesson, they are that much more memorable to you.

Sometimes, you may try to catch every word that the teacher says by trying to write it down frantically. At other times, you may use a lot of shorthand during lectures which may make your notes indecipherable later. Sometimes, you may not even bother with notes because you think you can remember the lecture and anyway, whatever is taught in class is bound to be in the textbook. At any rate, none of these techniques are effective enough to give you the best insight into the subject matter.

This is where Mind Mapping comes into play. When you use Mind Maps, you get a clearer idea of the content along with its relationship with other sub topics within the main topic. As you hear the lecture, keep drawing Mind Maps, starting at the centre and branching out. Since you are going to be drawing relationships and writing single words for ideas and sub topics, you will not be wasting time writing everything down verbatim. You will be able to see the topic in its entirety on one page and will not be wasting your energy in writing non-stop over endless pages. Since you will be making use of both the hemispheres of your brain, you will also be improving your analytic, logical, visual and imaginative skills, thereby increasing your brain power.

Pro Tip:

• Use Mind Maps to take down notes instead of writing them word for word or in shorthand.

Exercise 7: The 1, 12, 123 Method to learn the periodic table, poems and speeches.

When studying a long list, you begin with learning the first item, then you learn the first and second item, followed by the first, second and third item, and so on. The same method is followed when memorizing poems and speeches except that you go line by line. By the time you get to the end, you will be thorough with the whole list, poem, or speech. This method improves your brain's capacity to memorize things without too much of an effort.

Review this chapter and see if you can memorize the periodic table and the poem 'The Road Not Taken' by Robert Frost using this method. You can also look through your textbook or notebooks and memorize any long answers using this method.

SUMMARY

Memorizing a Second Language

- Learn through reading, writing, speaking, listening, watching movies, etc.
- Use the Nickname Method to associate the new word to its meaning and then convert this into images in your mind.
- This method can also be used to learn difficult words in English.

Memorizing Historic Events and Dates

- Use either the Number Shape Method or the Number Rhyme Method to remember the days of the month.
- Use Peg words to remember the months of the year and the Major System to remember the year.
- The entire list of dates and events can be remembered by using the Journey Method.
- A Mind Map may also be used to map out the entire list on one page in chronological order.

Learning the Periodic Table

- Use acrostics for the entire periodic table by learning all the elements in their respective groups.
- Once this is done, use the Journey Method to assign each group to a different location.
- Use the Nickname Method and Major System to link each element to their respective atomic numbers.

Learning Poems, Monologues and Speeches

- Use any of the Journey Methods to memorize poems, monologues and speeches.
- At every landmark, make an association between the landmark and the first word of the poem along with any key words in the sentence. Use these to form images in your mind.

Learning English Spellings

- Use the Nickname Method to form simple associations between the word to be learnt and its correct spelling. Make a sentence using the word in its correct context.
- When learning words that are spelled the same but pronounced differently, first learn the meanings of the words along with their pronunciations and then make simple sentences using the words in context.
- Use the Nickname Method and simple associations to help you spell commonly misspelled words.
- Learn irregular verbs that do not follow normal grammatical rules.

Effective Reading

- Learn to speed read by using your finger to guide your eyes while reading.

Effective Note-Taking

- Use Mind Maps to take down notes.

Chapter 8

Applying Memory Techniques in Daily Life

How to Remember Telephone Numbers and Other Long Numbers

You meet an old friend at a party and he gives you his phone number. You neither have a paper and pen to note it down, nor do you have your phone to store it in. How would you remember the number? Very often, phone numbers are stored in your short-term memory that lasts long enough to either write it down or dial the number. However, you may not be able to recall the number if asked for it a minute or two later, even if you have been repeating it in your mind before dialling. This is because numbers in general do not have particularly strong visual images in your mind and are usually meaningless. You can remember numbers better by applying any of the number systems such as the Number Shape System or Number Rhyme System or the Major System to the number that is to be remembered.

Let's take a ten-digit mobile phone number as an example—5897834129. Using the Number Shape System, you can convert this number into a seahorse, snowman, tennis racket, candy cane, snowman, heart, sailboat, candle, duck and tennis racket. Now using the Pure Link System, you can start your associations.

Seahorse and Snowman _____

Snowman and Tennis Racket _____

Tennis Racket and Candy Cane _____

Candy Cane and Snowman _____

Snowman and Heart _____

Heart and Sailboat _____

Sailboat and Candle _____

Candle and Duck _____

Duck and Tennis Racket _____

Alternatively, you can use the Story Link Method to put all the above words in a story to link them.

A **seahorse** and a **snowman** were playing with their **tennis rackets** when all of a sudden, a **candy cane** fell on the **snowman** and hit his **heart**. He then went on a **sailboat** where he lit a **candle** and met a **duck** who threw his **tennis racket** into the sea.

Using the Major System, how would you remember the same number? First you convert it into its peg letters.

5 8 9 7 8 3 4 1 2 9

Step 1—Convert—lf/v b/p c/k f/v m r t n p/b

The second step is to chunk these peg letters together and then add vowels to make them words. Since some numbers have more than one peg letter, choose the letter that you will be using.

Step 2—Chunk—lf bk fm rt np

Step 3—Add vowels and make words—**life book fam rat nip**.

Step 4—Story Link—The **Lifebook** called **FamRat** was **nip**ped.

Step 5—Convert back—Now simply recall these words—**life book fam rat nip**—and convert them back to their numbers of 5897834129.

Long Numbers

The Number Rhyme and Number Shape Systems may not be ideal for long numbers, so you can use the Major System. For example, let's take a random number such as 2847230481734. Using the Major System, convert this number into a more concrete image.

Step 1—Convert—The first step is to convert the number into its peg letters.

2 8 4 7 2 3 0 4 8 1 7 3 4
n f/v r k/c/g n m s/z r f/v t k/c/g m r

Step 2—Chunk—The next step is to break up the letters into chunks or groups. For numbers that have more than one letter, choose whichever letter you prefer. Here, the letter 'v' is used instead of 'f' for the number '8' and 'c' is used instead of 'k' for the number '7'.

Nvr   cn   msr   ft   cmr

Step 3—Add vowels and make words

Never   can   miser   fit   camera

Step 4—Story Link—Never can a miser fit a camera

Step 5—Convert back into numbers when required—Once you convert the phrase 'Never can a miser fit a camera' back into numbers, you get 2847230481734.

Let's try another example. This time, you will use random words from the Major System for the numbers and then use the Pure Link System or the Story Link System to remember the long number.

1 7 9 7 1 5 1 4 0 7 5 5 2 6 7 4 7 1 0 3

Step 1—Peg letters—t/d c/k/g b c/k/g t/d l t/d r s/z c/k/g l l n j/sh/ch c/k/g r c/k/g t/d s/z m

Letters used—d g b k t l d r s c l l n c h c r c t s m

Step 2—Chunked letters—dg bkt ldr scl lnch crkt sm

Step 3—Add vowels and make words—dog bucket ladder school

lunch cricket swim

Step 4—Pure Link System since words are unrelated

Dog and Bucket _____

Bucket and Ladder _____

Ladder and School _____

School and Lunch _____

Lunch and Cricket _____

Cricket and Swim _____

Story Link Method—A **dog** sleeps in a **bucket** that is being hauled up a **ladder** in **school** during **lunch** time while the **cricket** team **swim**.

Pro Tip:

As long as you remember the correct words in the above sentence in their correct order, you will be able to associate them back with their respective numbers and remember the original long number. While this seems to be a long process, once you get the hang of it, you will be able to translate numbers to words and phrases in an instant.

Exercise 1: Work out the following.

a) 3722910928449

   Peg letters _____

   Chunked letters _____

   Phrase _____

b) 001928374493039488

   Peg letters _____

   Chunked letters _____

   Phrase _____

c) 4839283749039485494030938789
   Peg letters _____
   Chunked letters _____
   Phrase _____

d) Write down any twenty-digit number using random numbers
   and see if you can recall it
   Peg letters _____
   Chunked letters _____
   Phrase _____

e) Your bank account number
   Peg letters _____
   Chunked letters _____
   Phrase _____

f) Your Aadhaar card number
   Peg letters _____
   Chunked letters _____
   Phrase _____

g) Your credit card number
   Peg letters _____
   Chunked letters _____
   Phrase _____

h) Your friend's cell phone number
   Peg letters _____
   Chunked letters _____
   Phrase _____

i) The value of pi—3.14159265358979323846
   Peg letters _____
   Chunked letters _____
   Phrase _____

j) The value of e (exponential function)—2.7182818
   Peg letters _____
   Chunked letters _____
   Phrase _____

Pro Tips:

- Try and make a sentence or phrase with the letters. If this is not possible, make words with the numbers and link them using either the Pure Link Method or the Story Link Method.
- Practice makes perfect! Whenever you see a long number, try and convert it. The more you practise, the faster you will be at converting any number into a memorable phrase or sentence.

Remembering Addresses

The same friend that you met at the party gives you his telephone number and his address and invites you to his apartment for lunch the next day. Remember, you don't have a paper, pen or your phone to record his address. How would you remember it? Here, you can use a combination of memory techniques. You can use the Nickname Method to remember the name of his apartment, the Number Rhyme or Number Shape Method to remember his door number and the Major System to remember his plot number. You can associate all the images using either the Pure Link Method or Story Link Method.

Let's assume that your friend's address is 302 Golden Enclave, No. 45/13 Gandhi Road. Using the Number Shape System, you convert the house number—302—into its associated shapes—heart, donut and duck. Using the Nickname Method, you can picture a giant apartment complex glimmering brightly in the sunlight because it is made of pure gold. 45/13 can be converted into its letters using the Major System—rl/tm, which can be further converted to **real time**. Of course, the image for Gandhi Road could be a vivid image of Mahatma Gandhi.

Story Link—when put all together and you get a **heart**-shaped **donut** being gobbled up by a **duck** inside a **golden** building glimmering brightly in the sun. You see Mahatma **Gandhi** in **real time** leading the way.

Once you have this image in your mind, you will not need a pen and paper or even your phone to remember it as it is easy enough to visualize it.

Exercise 2: Addresses

1. 915 Polo Apartments, Block B, 334 Basaveshwara Layout.
   915—Tennis racket + candle + seahorse (Number Shape)
   Polo Apartments—Round polo peppermint with a hole in the centre
   Block B—Bee (Alphabet rhyme)
   334—mmr—Memory
   Basaveshwara Layout—Bus + away + shhhhhh + war
   Story Link—A **tennis racket** lobbing a **candle** at a **seahorse** that is crunching down loudly on a **polo** peppermint. A **bee** is driving a bus away with a shhhhhh, off to war even though the war has ended because it has lost its **memory**.

2. No. 18, Sai Sangam, 7th Main, Banaswadi.
   181 _____
   Sai Sangam _____
   7th Main _____
   Banaswadi _____
   Story Link _____
   _____
   _____

3. Apartment 550, Serenity Towers, 889 Bandra.
   550 _____
   Serenity Towers _____
   889 _____
   Bandra _____
   Story Link _____
   _____
   _____

4. 99 Palm Acres, Phase 2, 15/90, Greater Kailash.
   99 _____
   Palm Acres _____
   Phase 2 _____
   15/90 _____
   Greater Kailash _____
   Story Link _____
   _____
   _____

5. 78 Fort Royale, Block D, 887 Millington Avenue.
   78 _____
   Fort Royale _____
   Block D _____
   887 _____
   Millington Avenue _____
   Story Link _____
   _____
   _____

6. 669 Akshay Apartments, Tower 8, 612 Connaught Place.
   669 _____
   Akshay Apartments _____
   Tower 8 _____
   612 _____
   Connaught Place _____

Pro Tips:

- You can mix and match any memory technique as long as you remember which memory technique you have used.
- As always, use the building blocks of visualization, association, imagination and location to see your images clearly.

Remembering Directions

Your friend has given you his telephone number and home address. Now he is giving you directions on how to reach his apartment from your home. Listen carefully and peg each direction using either the Number Shape System or the Number Rhyme System.

'Go straight till you reach Ulsoor Lake. From there, you come to a fork in the road. Take the middle road. At Garuda Shopping Mall, turn right. Go straight. At the second traffic light, take a left. You should see Vishnu Temple up ahead. Take the third turning to the left after Vishnu Temple. Golden Enclave is the third building from the main road.'

Now, let's see how to peg these directions to make them more memorable.

1. Bun—Ulsoor Lake
2. Shoe—Middle road on the fork.
3. Tree—Right turn at Garuda Shopping Mall.
4. Door—Left turn at second traffic light.
5. Hive—Third left turn after Vishnu Temple.
6. Sticks—Golden Enclave, third building from the main road.

Pure Links

1. Bun + Ulsoor Lake—A bun swimming in the lake and getting sore (Ulsoor).

2. Shoe + Middle road on the fork—Instead of road signs, there is a gigantic shoe pointing to the middle road near the lake.

3. Tree + Right turn at Garuda Shopping Mall—There is a tree that has fallen in front of Garuda Shopping Mall, blocking all other roads except the one on its right.

4. Door + Left turn at second traffic light _____
    _____

5. Hive + Third left turn after Vishnu Temple _____
    _____

6. Sticks + Golden Enclave, third building from the main road
    _____

Short Recall Test

1. Now that you've reached Golden Enclave, do you remember the apartment number?
2. Do you remember your friend's phone number?
3. What was the second direction that he gave you?
4. Golden Enclave is the _____ building from the main road.
5. What is the fifth direction that he gave you?

Pro Tips:

•   No matter how long the address, use any of the memory techniques to remember it. Some addresses may be as long as an essay (Tower 8, 2nd Cross, 5th Main, Door number 987), but you will still be able to remember them by using any or all of the memory techniques mentioned in this book.

•   These systems may seem long-winded but remember, while it may take pages to describe these systems, it takes only seconds to put them into practice.

•   Practice! Practice! Practice! The more you practise, the faster you will be at converting numbers, addresses and directions into memorable images.

Remembering Schedules and Appointments

You have already worked out an example for remembering schedules in the chapter on Number Rhyme Method. Try to work out one more example to remember your daily schedule in this chapter. Since you have now gone beyond the number system and have studied other memory techniques as well, you can combine any of the other techniques to remember your schedules and appointments.

Here's your schedule for the day. Using any of the memory techniques, try to memorize it.

8 a.m.—Fill petrol in bike

9 a.m.—Dentist Appointment

10 a.m.—Movie

1 p.m.—Lunch with friends

3 p.m.—Guitar classes

4 p.m.—Maths tuition

5 p.m.—pick up cricket jersey from school

5.30 p.m.—Interschool cricket match

8 p.m.—Scheduled episode of favourite TV show

9 p.m.—Revise one chapter of biology for upcoming exams before bed.

Since you have already used the Number Rhyme System to memorize schedules, use the Number Shape System to remember this list along with the Story Link Method to associate the time with the event in the schedule.

8 a.m. (Snowman) + Fill petrol in bike—There's a rock band called Snow Patrol so you might just need to remember the name of the group to remember the first task. However, if you are not

familiar with their music, another association may be a snowman riding his bike to the petrol bunk to fill it up with petrol but forgets and fills it up with snow instead.

9 a.m. (Tennis Racket) + Dentist Appointment—This one is going to be painful. Imagine a dentist knocking out all your teeth with a tennis racket!

10 a.m. (Girl + Hula Hoop) + Movie—You're watching a movie about a hula-hooping girl who beats all odds to become the world's number one hula-hooper!

1 p.m. (Candle) + Lunch with Friend—A nice candlelit lunch with all your friends.

3 p.m. (Heart) + Guitar Classes—Your guitar has suddenly become heart-shaped and plays only love songs!

4 p.m. (Sailboat) + Maths Tuition _____

_____

5 p.m. (Seahorse) + Pick Up Cricket Jersey from school _____

_____

5.30 p.m. (Seahorse + half another seahorse) + Inter-school cricket match _____

_____

8 p.m. (Snowman) + Favourite TV show _____

_____

9 p.m. (Tennis racket)—Revise one chapter of biology _____

_____

How do you distinguish between your tasks at 8 a.m. and 8 p.m. and also 9 a.m. and 9 p.m.? This is where contrast comes into play. When you picture your snowman riding your bike to the petrol bunk in the morning, make sure you see the sun shining brightly, reflecting off the bike and the petrol bunk and making your snowman melt. At 8 p.m., picture your snowman watching TV in pitch darkness. At 9 a.m., picture your dentist knocking out all your teeth with a tennis racket but also see this happening in bright daylight. At 9 p.m. when you are revising for your biology exam, picture doing it on your study table with a study lamp. This can be a clear indication of day and night.

Pro Tips:

- Use the Number Shape System or the Number Rhyme System to remember schedules and appointments.
- If you have the same number repeated signifying day and night, picture the event happening in bright sunlight or in complete darkness.

Remembering Birthdays, Anniversaries and Important Dates

To remember your friends' birthdays without relying on Facebook or online calendars to remind you, you can follow the same steps as described in chapter 7 to remember historic events and their dates. For this, you can follow the Nickname Method to associate your friend to his birthday, any of the Number Systems or the Major System to remember the date and the peg system of months to remember the month. Always write the day in dd/mm/yy format to avoid confusion. For birthdays and anniversaries, it may not be important to remember the year that your friend was born or the year that your parents got married so long as you remember the correct date, so that you can wish them. In the following examples, some are with the year and some without. Try and work out the last few examples by yourself.

1. Aakash's birthday is on 9 July.
   9—Tennis racket (Number Shape System)
   July—Umbrella
   Story Link—Imagine Aakash using a tennis racket like an umbrella and wondering why he's still getting wet in the rain.

2. Your parent's wedding anniversary is on 14 October.
   14—Tyre (Major System)
   October—Pumpkin
   Story Link—Picture a Halloween pumpkin on the front step of your parents' house. All of a sudden, a tyre rolls out of nowhere and rams into it, splashing pieces of pumpkin everywhere.

3. Your little sister Ayesha was born on 6 April 2008.
   6—Elephant's trunk
   April—Joker
   2008—nssf—**nose safe**
   Story Link—Ayesha sliding down an elephant's trunk, falling on a joker. But don't worry, her nose is safe.

4. Your best friend Seetha got married on 19 March 2018.
   19—Tub
   March—Question Papers
   2018—nstv—**nose TV**
   Seetha is sitting in a tub full of question papers in her wedding sari but all she can think of is how her nose will look on TV.

5. Your teacher tells you that your class tests will begin on 12 December 2018.
   12 _____
   December _____
   2018 _____

Story Link _____

_____

6. Your credit card will expire in May 2030.
   May _____
   2030 _____
   Story Link _____

   _____

7. Your passport is valid till 23 November 2037.
   23 _____
   November _____
   2037 _____
   Story Link _____

   _____

8. Your last date for college applications is 19 August 2018.
   19 _____
   August _____
   2018 _____
   Story Link _____

   _____

9. Your final exams start on 5 April 2019.
   5 _____
   April _____
   2019 _____
   Story Link _____

   _____

10. Your mother was born on 13 September 1955.
    13 _____
    September _____
    1955 _____

11. Your driver's licence expires on 30 January 2029.

30 _____

January _____

2029 _____

Pro Tips:

- Use the Number Shape Technique, the Number Rhyme Technique or the Major System to remember birthdays and other important dates. Peg the months to their corresponding image.
- Practically speaking, you need to remember the day and month more than the year, therefore you may skip the year when it comes to birthdays and anniversaries.
- This method can be used for any dates, including date of issue of passport, credit card expiry date, exam dates, etc. It can also be used for dates that are in the future.

Remembering Names

I'm at a party. Someone smiles at me and I smile back. I think I've seen this person before but where? The person comes up to me and exclaims, 'Shireeeen! Long time no see! How have you been?' I look at the person and smile thinly, replying 'Good! How have you been?' Since the person seems to know me well, it would be rude and downright insulting if I were to ask the person who she is. I therefore pretend that I know her and maintain polite conversation for a few more minutes before I excuse myself and move on.

Most people are terrible at remembering names although they're not as bad at remembering faces. Even if you are not able to recall a person's face once they are out of your sight, you will still be able to recognize them the next time you see them. This is because you can see a face but you can't see a name. A name is abstract—just syllables and sounds bunched together to form other sounds. A face is more concrete—something that you can see, touch and feel. Since your mind remembers pictures better than sounds, you would naturally remember a face better than a name.

A person's name is their identity. Remembering someone's name is a great way to make them feel important and recognized and also helps you build long lasting connections with them. This might sound a little trite but a person's name is his most prized possession and there is nothing more pleasing to him than hearing his own name or being remembered by others. Chalk it down to human nature, but you automatically feel positive towards people who call you by name and remember your name after meeting you just once or when meeting you after many years.

How would you feel if a friend or someone you have known for a long time called you by the wrong name? How embarrassed would you be if someone knew your name but you couldn't remember theirs? The following are a few strategies to remember names *without* using memory techniques. By following these strategies alone, you will be able to increase your retention of names by at least 50 per cent. You can work on the other 50 per cent by using memory techniques discussed later in this chapter.

1. **Pay Attention**—When someone is being introduced to you or someone tells you their name, pay attention to it at the very beginning. Don't get distracted by all the social niceties such as shaking hands, kissing cheeks, hugging, etc. You cannot remember a name that you didn't take the trouble to absorb in the first place. Even if you're sure that you will never meet this person again, pay attention to his name.

2. **Self-fulfilling Prophecy**—Don't have the attitude of, 'Anyway I'll never see him again so why bother?' or 'What a name! I'll

never remember it in a hundred years!' or 'I'm bad at names anyway.' These thoughts become self-fulfilling prophecies and because you think 'I'm bad at names' or 'My memory sucks,' you will automatically stop trying or making the effort to remember names. Instead, have a more positive attitude of, 'New names and people are always interesting' or 'I will make the effort to remember this person's name' or 'I can do it!'

3. **Ask**—If you did not hear the name clearly, ask the person to repeat it. If it is an unusual name and difficult to pronounce, try repeating it after the person till you get the pronunciation right. Many people hesitate to ask someone to repeat their name but there's no harm in saying, 'Sorry, would you mind repeating that?' In fact, people are generally flattered when you take an interest in their name. Don't be embarrassed to ask someone their name.

4. **Spell**—If you still didn't get the name after you asked the person to repeat and pronounce it, you can ask them to spell it. Better yet, try and spell it yourself! If you make a mistake, the other person will correct you but spelling the name yourself will leave a more lasting impression of it on your mind. For example, you meet someone named Catherine, you know that Catherine has many spellings such as Catheryn, Katherine, Catherin, Kathryn, etc. so just to be sure, ask her if it is spelled with a C or a K or whether there is an I or a Y at the end. Since people may have been misspelling her name her whole life, she would be glad that someone is actually taking the trouble to find out the right spelling.

5. **Familiar name**—After finding out the spelling, you may realize that the name is similar to someone you know or are related to. Mention this and it will form another lasting impression on your mind.

6. **Unique name**—If it is a unique name that you have never heard before, mention that as well. As discussed earlier, it is human nature to be flattered when someone makes a fuss over your name, so even the small mention of you thinking it to be a unique name will strengthen the connection between you and the person whose name you've just heard.

7. **Meaning**—If the name is a unique name, ask the person to spell it out for you and then ask them the meaning of their name. You can say something like, 'What a nice name! What does it mean?' You can also follow up this question with one on the origin of the name. 'Where does your name come from?' 'Shireen' is a Persian name. It means 'sweet'. This of course, can serve as an effective ice-breaker and can lead to further conversation.

8. **Grouping same names**—If it is a common name and you know many people who have the same name, have a gathering in your mind where you put everybody with the same name in one room, including the person you have just met. So, if you know a few people named Ajay, Arun, Debbie, Smitha, Anita, etc., picture all the 'Ajays' in one room, all the 'Aruns' in another, and all the 'Debbies' in a separate room. In future, when you remember this image and remember placing this new person in a room full of 'Anitas', you will automatically recall that her name is Anita.

9. **Repeat the name at appropriate places**—While talking to the person, repeat the name as often as you can during the course of the conversation. Insert the new person's name wherever applicable, perhaps at important points in the conversation. Avoid using their name consistently or the conversation may get weird. For example, 'Nice to meet you, Jeffrey Summers. What kind of artist are you, Jeffrey? Do you travel a lot, Jeffrey? Do you know a lot of people at this party, Jeffrey?'

This is not only annoying, but also sounds a bit fake, don't you think?

10. **Introduce**—If you are joined by another friend, make sure you introduce him to your new acquaintance by using their full names if possible, along with a snippet of information about them to further the conversation. This shows that you've been paying attention to the conversation thus far. For example, 'Sammy, I'd like you to meet Jeffrey Summers. Jeff is an artist! Jeff, this is Samuel Peters. Sammy plays the drums in our band.' Sometimes, the person making the introduction may remember only *your* name but not the other person's name. The introduction may therefore be a little one-sided and may go something like, 'This is my good friend Sally.' In this case, don't be afraid to follow up with, 'Nice to meet you. Sorry, I didn't quite catch your name.'

11. **Use the name while saying goodbye**—When you part ways, don't just mumble something generic like 'It was nice meeting you. Hope to see you again soon.' Make it a little more personal by using the person's name. 'It was nice meeting you today, Catherine. Let's catch up again soon!'

12. **Ask for a business card**—If the opportunity presents itself, ask the person for his or her business card. This is especially useful since it gives you the opportunity to look at the written name and the face at the same time, thereby making a visual link in your memory.

13. **Interest**—Take a genuine interest in the people you meet. By following the above strategies, you make names interesting, you act interested and in so doing, you actually create interest. And, since interest is a large part of memory, you will also be honing your memory skills and training your brain to be excited about learning something new.

14. **Consolidation**—After you have moved on, take a minute to

recall the name of the person that you just met. Repeat to yourself the person's name, the spelling, the meaning, any background material that you have gathered about the name or the person to whom it belongs. These associations will further strengthen your memory and deepen the encoding.

Pro Tips:

- Make an effort to practise this proactively with every new person that you meet. At first, it may seem like an effort but the more you practise, the more it becomes a part of the way you interact and it will make your communication skills and interpersonal skills better. Memory for names gets worse over time, so practice is the key.

- All the above strategies will increase your memory for names by 25–50 per cent if you keep practising them.

- Stop saying 'I'm sorry, I'm bad with names.' Instead, reinforce positives in your mind by saying 'I can and shall make the effort to remember names.'

Remembering Faces

Since you can actually see a face, you do not need to utilize visualization techniques to remember it. Pay close attention to the features of a person's face. As mentioned earlier, attention is the key to remembering anything. If you don't pay attention, the information does not enter your system to begin with and therefore, you will never be able to remember it.

Imagine that you were a witness to a crime and you had to describe the criminal to the police sketch artist. While the physical build of the criminal, his height, skin and hair colour, visible tattoos, etc., are important, describing his face in great detail is of the utmost importance. How would you go about doing this? Would you be able to describe the criminal's eyes?

What about the shape of his face? Apart from the colour and length, was there anything else that was distinctive about his hair?

Thankfully, meeting new people is not as stressful as having to describe a criminal to the police but remembering their faces is just as important to avoid embarrassment in future. Here are a few facial features that you can pay special attention to. Do note that while it is alright to observe spectacles, clothing and jewellery, these can be changed or replaced and therefore do not serve as good memory aids. Similarly, some skin conditions such as pimples are temporary and may not be there the next time you see the person and, therefore, are not used as memory aids.

Shape—Notice the shape of a person's face. Some common shapes are heart-shaped, rectangular, oval, round and square-shaped. Some people may have a kite-shaped face, which means that they have prominent cheek bones which are wide and their face narrows towards their chin. Some people may have a face in the shape of a teardrop, which means that the face may be shorter on top with a forehead that is narrower than the cheekbones. A rare facial shape is the oblong shape where the face is longer and wider at the forehead, cheekbones as well as chin and jawline.

Eyes—The eyes of a person are memorable features. You may be able to remember a person's eyes better if you have maintained eye contact while talking and noticed what colour they were, whether they were set too close or far apart from their nose, whether they were deep set or bulging in their face, whether they were narrow or wide, whether they were looking yellowish or they had bags under them due to lack of sleep, whether they were bright and intelligent, or sparkling with mischief…the list goes on. Notice the area around the eyes. Does the person have laugh lines or crow's feet near the corner of their eyes? Is there anything distinct about the eye lashes? Are the eyelids droopy?

Is one eye larger than the other? Is there a slight squint?

Eyebrows—Eyebrows can be bushy, thin, arched or even scarce. Some people have a unibrow, which means that both eyebrows meet in the middle above the nose or they may even be drawn in to define them better.

Hair—Hairstyles and hair colour and length can constantly change. Sometimes, even the nature of hair might change. For example, a person with straight hair might perm it and make it curly (or vice versa). Men could either grow a beard or moustache or shave it off. Since hair is ever-changing, it may not be a good idea to use this as a memory aid unless there is something outstanding or unique about the person's hair.

Nose—A person's nose can be bulbous, long and pointed, short and flat, button-shaped, turned up, crooked, wide, narrow, etc. Nostrils can be flared or narrow or even hairy.

Teeth—Teeth can be straight, crooked, decaying, have silver caps, be yellowish, chipped, sticking out at odd angles or absolutely perfect. Some people may wear braces while in some cultures, it is common to replace regular teeth with gold teeth!

Mouth and ears—Notice the shape of the mouth, lips and ears. Does the person have a wide mouth? Pouty mouth? Thin lips? Cracked or dry lips? Are his ears protruding or pierced?

Skin—Skin colour and tone vary. Especially in a diverse country like India, skin colour often catches the eye first. Skin can be smooth or wrinkled. Some people may even have visible tattoos or birthmarks. Acne such as pimples and dark spots may be visible.

Smile and laugh—While a smile gets encoded in your visual memory, a laugh gets encoded in your auditory memory. A smile can completely transform a person's face. Observe if the smile is genuine or fake, whether the smile is crooked or straight, whether it is shy or bold, etc. Observe if a person's laugh is high pitch or comes in short bursts, is loud and carefree or soft and guarded, etc.

Voice—Listen to the voice. Observe if it is high-pitched, deep, booming, musical, squeaky, hoarse, bright, uplifting, deadpan, dry, etc.

Other characteristics—There may be wrinkles on the forehead, or dimples on the cheeks or near the lips. Some people have a cleft chin or a 'chin dimple' while others have a deep grove in the space just below the nose and above the upper lip. Some people may have moles or beauty spots on their face.

Sometimes, it may be hard to distinguish people of other races or ethnicities from each other. This is because people from other races are seen as a group rather than as individuals. For example, you may say that 'all Asians look alike' but this is because you see Asians as a group rather than as individuals who have their own distinct features. By noticing the features described above, you will be able to distinguish quite easily between one Asian and another.

When applying memory techniques, you need to focus on one aspect of the face that is unique to that person or is a distinguishing factor. For example, when you think of Jay Leno, the talk show host, you immediately notice his prominent chin. When you look at Donald Trump, what would strike you first is the orange colour of his skin. When you look at George Clooney, you might be struck by the absolute symmetry of his face, however, think of one distinctive facial feature that might make him distinguishable from say Brad Pitt. Mahatma Gandhi is represented on Indian currency notes and in the 'Swachh Bharat Abhiyan' movement by the distinctive round spectacles that he wore.

When remembering faces, don't just focus on facial features alone but try to exaggerate the feature as much as you can to make the face more memorable. Does the person have a heart-shaped face? Exaggerate the face so that it becomes a gigantic heart with a tiny body attached. If the person has wide eyes, exaggerate the eyes and make them as big as saucers. If the person has a tattoo on his skin, animate it to make it pulse or jump around doing tricks. If the person has crooked or chipped teeth, imagine how that happened. Did he bite into a large rock? Did he walk into a wall?

Pro Tips:
- Pay attention to facial features.
- Notice the prominent features and exaggerate.
- Make the exaggeration as rude or ridiculous as possible to remember the person better. There's no need to tell the person what technique you are using.

Memory Techniques to Remember Names and Faces

Names and faces can be a fun observation exercise. Look at remembering names and faces as a game and have fun playing. Here are a few fun memory techniques to remember names and faces.

Rhymes—Rhyming a name with something else can be a fun way of remembering names. In my case, I was always called Shireen the Baked Bean in school. Not that I was particularly fond of beans, baked or otherwise, it was just one of the very few words that could actually be rhymed with my name. Rhymes can be based on the person's physique, hobbies, job, temperament or any other distinguishing feature that they may have such as mannerisms, etc. For example, Miss Pich likes to stitch, or Shekhar is a good baker, or Vase Srinivas or Fair Clare or Plain Jane, etc. When meeting a person for the first time, you are likely to remember their name better if you rhyme it with something else.

Songs—Some people have songs that have their names in them so just by remembering a snippet of the song, you'll automatically remember their names. Names such as Sarah, Sharona, Maria, Mary, Jane, Billy, Johnny, etc. are common in songs. So, if you were to meet someone named Maria, you might have the song 'How Do You Solve a Problem Like Maria' from the movie *The Sound of Music* playing in your head every time you thought about her. If you met someone named Mary, you might wonder where her little lamb was. If you met a Billy, you may have Michael Jackson's 'Billie Jean' playing in your head. You may probably have Bon Jovi's 'Janie Don't You Take Your Love to Town' running through your head every time you thought of Jane. If it is a unique name, rhyme it with an existing name from a song. For example, if you were to meet a girl named Sharola, you may rhyme it with Sharona and therefore the song 'My Sharona' by The Knack would be associated with her. If there are no existing songs or no songs that rhyme with the name, make up your own.

Personal meaning—'Hi, my name is Pinky.' Ah, same name as the teddy bear that I used to have when I was little, I think. Since I used to carry that teddy bear with me everywhere I went and I was quite attached to it as a little girl, I will never forget the name Pinky. Associating names with something familiar or personal will help burn the name into your memory so you never forget it. This happens because you are using one of the memory building blocks of association where you are associating something new with something that you are already familiar with. Since what you are associating already exists in your long-term memory, it becomes easier to remember the name in future.

Personal associations need not be confined to just names alone. For example, in a room full of people, you are bound to share your birthday or at least your birth month with one other person. Don't you think you would remember this person's name better if you shared the same birthday? Always look for associations. The more random the association (Look! We both have tattoos on our neck!), the better you will remember the name and face.

Nickname Method Based on Meaning

You can use the Nickname Method to remember names as you have done in previous chapters. The following are nicknames that are derived from the meanings of the names themselves. Simply remembering the meaning of names might not be enough to remember the name later. You will need to make the meanings come alive themselves. To do this, use the Story Link Method to associate the meaning to the real name of the person. The first few are worked out for you. Try and work out the rest.

Name	Meaning	Story Link
Kamal	Lotus	Kamal snoring loudly on a bed made of lotuses.
Bahadur	Brave	Lal Bahadur Shastri bravely fighting for India's freedom.
Shifrah	Beautiful	Shifrah looked beautiful with her long hair flowing in waves.
Adele	Noble	Adele (the singer) had a concert for a noble cause.
Sabah	Morning	Sabah looking grumpy in the morning.
Shanthi	Peace	

Annika	Graceful	
Luke	Light	
Heera	Diamond	
Nadiya	River	

The above story links could also be made keeping a facial characteristic in mind. For example, you may think that Kamal snores loudly because you noticed that his nose was red and stuffy since he had a cold. Shifrah's long hair flowing in waves could be a direct and obvious reference to her long, beautiful hair. Linking the meaning of the name to a facial characteristic or a distinguishing characteristic is also a good way to remember names as you will see later in this chapter.

Nickname Method Based on Association

Some names automatically trigger memories or associations with famous people, movies, songs, countries, rivers, mountain ranges, gods, etc. For example, the name America Ferrera (the actress who plays Betty in *Ugly Betty*) has an obvious association with America and therefore, just by associating her with America, you will remember her name. Another example would be John Smith. Now, this is a common name and there must be a few million John Smiths all over the world, but if you notice that he bears a slight resemblance to the actor Johnny Depp, the next time you meet John Smith, you will remember Johnny Depp and therefore be able to remember his name. You can use associations for either the first name or the surname. However, since you will be using a person's first name more than his surname, try and make associations with only the first name.

Name	Association	
Bahadur Sinha	Lal Bahadur Shastri	2nd Prime Minister of India
Rabin Rao	Rabindranath Tagore	Indian Poet
Ethan Tanner	Ethan Hunt	Character from *Mission Impossible* films
Bruce Edwards	Bruce Springsteen	Singer, Musician
Kavery Kanna	Cauvery River	River
Rajeev Sharma		
Seetha Manoj		
Sunil Bhatt		
Taylor Stephen		
Tom Morris		

Nickname Method Based on Sound

If the names and surnames are long and/or complicated, you can break them up into their sounds and then use the sounds to form associations. Let's take a few long and complicated names and work with them. Don't worry about the spelling. You are only going to look at the pronunciations as you need to remember these people by name the next time you see them.

Name	Sound
Okello Akinyi (Tanzania) (F)	Oh! Kell oh! Aching eee!
Kalaivani Anbuselvan (Tamil Nadu, India) (F)	Kala + Van + Ee + Ambulance + Sell + van
Hemakshi Bapodra (Gujarat, India) (F)	Hem + Akshee + Baroda

Hristiyan Kyolcheski (Macedonia) (F)	Wrist + Yank + Yowl + Chest + Ski
Lars Grimsby (Norway) (M)	Mars + Grims + Bee
Ratna Jayawardene (Sri Lanka) (M)	Rat + no + Jaya + War + Dean
Jostein Gustavsson (Sweden) (M)	Yo + Sting + Gust + of + Sun
Gabriela Zagbayou (Ivory Coast) (F)	Gab + Reel + Aaah + Zag + Bay + You
Guillaume Charbonnier (France) (M)	Gill + Arm + Sharp + On + Air (sharpener)
Gökmen Özdemir (Turkey) (M)	Gawk + men + Oz + Them + Ere

Associating Names to Faces

Continue with the list above and see how you can remember the names of these people when you see them in person.

Okello Akinyi—Meet Okello Akinyi, a young Tanzanian girl. As you can see, the distinguishing feature of her face is her large forehead. Remember her name by the sound Oh Kell Oh Aching Eee, as described above. Now, peg the sound of her name onto her distinguishing facial feature—her large forehead. Imagine her forehead throbbing with pain and Okello complaining saying, 'Oh Kell Oh! How it's aching! Eee!'

Hristiyan Kyolcheski—This is Hristiyan Kyolcheski from Macedonia. Her distinguishing feature is her deep dimples. Her name sounds like Wrist + Yank + Yowl + Chest + Ski. How can you associate her name to her dimples? You may picture her wrist being yanked. It hurts so much that she yowls from her chest and skis down the slopes of her deep dimples.

Lars Grimsby—This is Lars Grimsby from Norway. Lars rhymes with Mars so you can go with Mars as an association for his name. As you can see, he has a thick beard, however, a beard can be easily shaved off or modified and so it would be difficult to use it as a permanent peg. Hmm. What about his bushy eyebrows? He's not likely to shave those off! So, going by the sound of his name, you have Mars + Grims + Bee. A bee is sitting on Lars' bushy eye brows and grimly contemplating flying to Mars.

Ratna Jayawardene—This is Ratna Jayawardene from Sri Lanka. He is recognizable by his thick spectacles. While spectacles are not usually used as pegs because they can be changed, he has informed you that due to some problem with his eyes, he can never wear contact lenses. The spectacles therefore will be a permanent feature on his face. His name is broken down into Rat + No + Jaya + War + Dean. Imagine a rat screaming 'No war! No war!' to his friends Jaya and Dean. Imagine the Rat, Jaya and Dean peering

at each other short-sightedly through their thick spectacles.

Kalaivani Anbuselvan—Meet Kalaivani, a girl from Tamil Nadu, India. As you can see, her distinguishing feature is her long, thick, brown hair. Since it is a Tamil custom to have long hair, there may be no danger of her cutting it short any time soon so you can use her hair as her distinguishing feature. Her name broken up into its sounds is Kala (black) + Van + Ee + Ambulance + Sell + Van, which you need to peg to her long black hair. Imagine a 'kala' (black) van going 'Eeee' because it is actually an Ambulance van that you had to sell. Imagine this black ambulance winding up her long black hair going 'Eeeee!'

Hemakshi Bapodra—This is Hemakshi from Baroda, Gujarat. Picture Hem making this sound when she sneezes—aksheee—instead of achoooo, and the whole of Baroda can hear it. As you can see, she has beautiful tear-drop eyes. So picture Hem sneezing 'Aksheee! Aksheee!' So much that her eyes start watering.

Guillaume Charbonnier—This is Guillaume Charbonnier from the South of France. His distinguishing features are his long face and his long, sharp nose. His name is broken into Gill + Arm + Sharpener. Imagine him having a gill instead of an arm. Picture how it would look if he were to hold a sharpener in his gills and uses it to sharpen his long nose.

Jostein Gustavsson—This is Jostein Gustavsson of Sweden. His prominent facial feature is his massive jawline. His name is broken down into Yo + Sting + Gust + of + Sun. Just as you would imagine a gust of wind, imagine a gust of sunlight hitting him on his jawline and stinging him!

Gökmen Özdemir—This is Gökmen Özdemir from Turkey. As you can see, his distinguishing feature is his cleft chin which is as attractive and enviable as Hristiyan Kyolcheski's deep dimples. His name can be broken up into Gawk + Men. Imagine all men gawking at his cleft chin.

Gabriela Zagbayou—This is Gabriela Zagbayou from the Ivory Coast. As you can see, her prominent features are her large ears. Her name is broken into Gab + Reel + Aaah + Zag + Bay + You. Imaging her gabbing all the time and reeling off story after story. Would it make you go 'Aaah!' Imagine her gabbing so much that her ears start becoming bigger and bigger to accommodate all those stories. Here, even though her last name is not taken into account (you can if you want), you will still remember her first name by picturing her reeling from gabbing so much and you going 'Aaah!'

Remembering Names through Locations

You can apply real or imagined locations to help you memorize names. The thumb rule for any memory aid is to visualize your image at a particular location. This helps give your image some context and it is not just floating in air in your mind.

A real location would be where you know the person from. For example, Anita from ballet class or Priya from Hindi tuitions. If you happened to see Anita at a mall, your mind would automatically place her in her ballet costume inside the ballet class and you would then remember her name. Likewise for Priya. If you saw her at a different location, say a movie theatre, you may be wondering where you had seen her before. As soon as you place her at the correct location of Hindi tuitions, you will remember that her name is Priya.

When it is difficult to associate someone at a particular location, you can imagine a location for them. For example, you go to a party and you meet a number of people there. Later, you may remember 6–7 names but you would recall all of them in the same location and this may mix up the names in your mind. To avoid this, you can imagine locations for each person that you meet. You can use locations based on their looks, their jobs or something they've said during the course of the conversation. For example, you meet a smart young girl with intelligent eyes and a clear way of articulating her thoughts. Her name is Lauren Chambers. Just by the way she talks you think she may make a good lawyer. And what a coincidence—her name is Law-ren Chambers! You can therefore picture Lauren dressed up in her lawyer's robes, sitting in her chambers and arguing cases clearly. She may not actually be a lawyer but your visualization will help you remember her name the next time you meet her.

Let me introduce you to Barry Larson. As you talk to Barry, you are struck by how deep and rich his voice is. You think that he could be an amazing singer and could probably sing bass as his voice is so deep. You place him in a church choir. You can break up Barry's name into Baritone (bass) and Lark. So, your association for him would be a Lark named Barry, singing in a rich baritone in the church choir.

Mental Snapshot Method

Remember the three basic rules for the Mental Snapshot Method—look, snap and connect.

When you meet a person for the first time, take a visual snapshot of the person's face. This is called the 'face snap'. To do this, first identify a feature that may be distinguishing or distinctive to that person. Usually, the extraordinary feature that you notice first is what you will remember later.

Next, create a person's name snap using any of the nickname methods mentioned above.

The third step is to connect the face snap to the name snap of the person, in your mind. This is done by using the 'Associating Names to Faces' method discussed above. Once you have a visual image of the person along with her name and can see it clearly in your mind, you have your Mental Snapshot. Add a location to this person, whether real or imagined, and you will have the image of the person 'burnt' into your mind, never to be forgotten.

Pro Tips:

When you meet or are introduced to someone new:

- Make sure that you pay attention and take interest in learning the name at the beginning of the conversation itself.
- Have a clear mental image of the name.
- Peg the name to some facial characteristic or distinguishing feature.

- Associate the sound or meaning of the name with that distinguishing feature.
- Once the meeting is over, review the person's name, facial characteristics and any other pieces of information and associate them all to the person.
- As mentioned earlier, while it may take a few pages to describe these techniques, it takes only a second or two to picture these associations in your mind.
- Most of the time, in social situations, you only need to remember a person's first name. So it is alright if you do not do the association for the surname. In an official setting, you may need to remember the surname more than the first name as you will need to call the person say Mr Özdemir rather than Gökmen. In this case, putting more emphasis on the sound of the surname may be more important. In an official setting where you need to remember the name of a client, customer, vendor, etc. it helps to remember both the first name and surname.
- To remember just the name, look for associated sounds. To peg the name to the face, look for distinguishing facial characteristics and then peg the sounds of the name to that characteristic.
- Don't worry about the spellings. It's the pronunciation that matters. If you feel that the spellings matter, there is no harm in asking the person to spell his name or to ask the person for his business card.
- Add sound bites or sound effects wherever possible. For example, Gabriela gabbing and you thinking 'Aaah!' or the ambulance going 'Eeee!' for Kalaivani.
- While only facial characteristics in association with names have been discussed, you can peg names to any other characteristic such as mannerisms, speech defects,

type of clothing, birth marks, or the person's job.

- Use the same techniques to remember historical figures by looking at a picture of them and tagging their names to some distinguishing characteristic. If there is no picture, imagine what the person would look like based on his deeds and actions. For example, Jahangir was a great warrior. Even though there is no picture of him, you can still imagine him standing tall with a sword in one hand.

Exercise 1: Name Test

Read through the names and descriptions given earlier and then focus on the following faces. Identify them and write down their names.

Exercise 2: Face Test

Here's the list of names discussed above. Next to each name, write down the distinguishing facial characteristic. Try not to look at the pictures above, rather try to picture the names and associated faces in your mind.

Name	Distinguishing Facial Characteristic
Jostein Gustavsson	Big jawline
Gökmen Özdemir	
Gabriela Zagbayou	
Lars Grimsby	
Guillaume Charbonnier	
Ratna Jayawardene	
Kalaivani Anbuselvan	
Okello Akinyi	
Hristiyan Kyolcheski	
Hemakshi Bapodra	

Finding Lost Objects

'*I once spent more than half an hour hunting for my glasses only to realize I was wearing them the whole time!*'

'*I can never find my keys.*'

'*I'm always late in the mornings because I can never find my wallet!*'

'*I once turned my whole house upside down looking for the TV remote control, only to find it in the freezer!*'

'*I know I kept those diamond earrings in a safe place. I just don't remember where!*'

I'm sure you've had some of the above experiences at least once in the last six months. Some of you may have had these at least once or twice on a daily basis! The reason is quite obvious. It is because you fail to pay attention to what you are doing at that moment. This could be because you are distracted with something else, you are multitasking or preoccupied, or you are doing things mechanically without really thinking about it.

Some people mistake absent-mindedness for a bad memory but it is just that—an absence of mindfulness. If you are more mindful of or pay attention to where you keep your things, you will not waste much time finding them simply because you will be aware of where they are. Follow the thumb rule—you can't remember what you didn't pay attention to in the first place. So, the first technique to mindfulness and repairing absent-mindedness is to pay attention to what you are doing at all times.

You've lost your spectacles and can't find them. How can you remember where they are? The second technique is to follow the sequence of events in a forward direction. You know you definitely had them on at some point today. Start with that point.

You were sitting on the sofa in the living room and reading the newspaper this morning. You were definitely wearing your spectacles at that point or you would not have been able to read anything. While reading, you were sipping your coffee and then you went into the kitchen to wash the cup. Since these are reading glasses, you would have taken them off before going to the kitchen. So they must be somewhere in your living room near the sofa. Ah! You've found them under the newspaper! Good job!

Here's another scenario. You need to pay your electricity bill. Every day, you keep forgetting to take the bill with you and you remember this only after you leave the house. Finally, you decide to put the bill inside your wallet but again, it may sit in your wallet for the next few days with no action taken because you keep forgetting to go to the electricity office. In a case like this, you can use the association technique to link the last thing that you do when you leave the house, to the electricity bill. So, if the last thing that you do is put your shoes on, link this action to the action of paying the electricity bill. Perhaps visualize putting on your shoes and they suddenly bite you, screeching 'Bill! Bill! Bill!' If you have decided to pay the bill after school, associate the last thing you do in school to the electricity bill. Perhaps the last thing that you do is get on your cycle. Picture blocking out every other road except the road that leads from school to the electricity office. You get on your cycle and that is the only road that you can take because all other roads are blacked out. Have a huge neon sign on top of the electricity office that flashes: 'Pay here! Pay here!'

A fourth technique that can be used is the mental snapshot technique. You know that you are keeping your diamond earrings in a 'safe place'. It may help you to take a mental snapshot of this safe place so that you don't forget it later. To do this, pay special attention to where you are storing it and look at the objects around. For example, say you have put your diamond earrings in a small cream-coloured jewellery box and you're hiding this little box in the right-hand far corner of your wardrobe behind your saris. Since you usually put your jewellery in a large wooden box, you look at this cream-coloured box and take a snapshot of it in your mind. After you hide it behind your saris, you take another mental snapshot of that corner of your wardrobe and then associate the saris to your diamond earrings. This way, when you think of your diamond earrings, you will have two mental snapshots—one showing the location and one showing the new container.

You may often worry about whether you have left the gas, or the iron, or the geyser on. Sometimes, you may even come back home to check if you have switched off all these appliances. A fifth technique for absent-mindedness is to simply close your eyes and try to remember yourself shutting off all these appliances. If you can picture turning off the gas or pulling out the plug of the iron while wearing the clothes that you are wearing right now, then chances are very high that you have actually done these things.

A sixth technique to use if you have forgotten something is to review what you *can* remember. For example, if you have forgotten one or two items that were part of a list, review the other items on the list. Sometimes, reading the other items may trigger an association with the forgotten item. Sometimes, even the position of the other items on the list may offer a clue as to what the forgotten item may be.

If you have been trying very hard to remember something and all the above techniques have failed, take your mind off it and think about something else. Sometimes, the harder you try to remember something, the more elusive it becomes. Often, the answer will just 'pop into your mind' when you least expect it simply because while your conscious mind has been focussing on something else, your sub-conscious has been working on remembering but it might need a tiny nudge in the form of some association to trigger the memory. For example, you meet someone whose name you cannot remember. The more you try to remember the person's name, the more you come up blank. Sometime later (maybe a few hours or at times even a few days later), perhaps when you are gardening you suddenly remember that the person's name is Rose!

Pro Tips:

- Make it a habit to be aware of every little thing that you do.
- The first technique is to pay attention to everything that you do. You cannot expect to remember something if you haven't

paid attention to it in the first place.

- The second technique is to start at the point where you had the object last and work your way forward from there.
- The third technique is to associate the last thing that you do before you leave the house with the chore that needs to be done.
- The fourth technique is the mental snapshot one.
- The fifth technique is simply to close your eyes and try to recollect if you have done something in particular such as switch off an electrical appliance.
- If you forget an item on a list, review other items in case one of them sparks off an association.
- If you've forgotten something, think about something else. Sometimes the information you are trying to remember will just 'pop up' in your mind at some later time.
- Making these deliberate associations with small, everyday things will improve your memory and save you the time it takes to look for things.

Remembering Dreams

Some people think that they dream too much while other people think that they never dream at all. Some people remember their dreams in vivid detail while others just have a blurred impression of having dreamed but no specific image. The good news is that everybody dreams. The better news is that you can remember your dreams by using some of the memory techniques that you have learnt.

The first step in dream memory is to remember the dream itself. This can be done by shifting your mindset to be more positive just before you go to sleep. Once you settle in for the night and close your eyes, gently but firmly repeat a mantra, 'I will remember my dreams.' This will program your brain to remember your dreams when you wake up. The disclaimer here is that it may take as many as three to four weeks before you can clearly remember a dream but this is the time it takes to 'program' your brain.

Once you have a dream in mind, it is important to not get too excited or it may just slip away from your conscious mind. Your brain needs to be in a 'non-excited' state to be able to calmly remember details of the dream. If you tax it or overthink at this stage, you might run the risk of implanting false memories in your dreams as well. So, the second step is to keep calm and review your dream from beginning to end.

The next step is to be able to recall the dream in its correct order of sequence. To do this, you can use any of the Number Systems or Alphabet Systems to peg the dream in its correct order. For example, you dreamt that you were walking along the road and suddenly you saw a field of golden sunflowers that stretched as far as the eye can see. All of a sudden, you see something bouncing on the sunflowers in the distance. As you squint your eyes, you realize that there are gigantic elephants bouncing from one sunflower to the next! One elephant invites you to join them in their endless bouncing!

You can use the Number Rhyme System to peg the sequence of your dream. So, imagine a road running through a gigantic bun (one). Next, you see golden sunflowers inside your shoe (two)... and so on, till you have recorded your whole dream.

It helps to keep a notebook and pen right next to your pillow so that you can jot down your dreams as soon as you wake up. Dreams are usually fresh when you wake up but quickly fade from memory a few minutes later. It helps to 'catch' these dreams while they are still fresh in your mind. Write down the dream as you remember it. Don't try to put in meanings or worry about symbolisms just yet. Once you have written down or remembered the whole dream, you can look at it and see if it means anything to you. This will not only help your memory but will also help your literary and writing skills.

Studies have shown that people who start remembering their dreams are calmer, more motivated, humorous, imaginative and are better at remembering things in general. Since dreams happen while you are asleep, remembering them while you are awake connects your conscious mind to your subconscious mind and exercises your cognitive skills. Getting in touch with these skills on a conscious level encourages all the connected skills to improve automatically.

Pro Tips:

- Use positive reinforcement in the form of a mantra on yourself. Once you program your brain to remember dreams, you will find it easier to remember them.
- Review your dreams with a calm mind. If you get over-excited, you might forget the dream.
- Use any of the memory systems to remember your dream in order.
- Keep a notebook and pen next to your pillow and write down the dream as soon as you wake up.

SUMMARY

How to Remember Telephone Numbers and Long Numbers

- Use the Number Shape Method or the Number Rhyme Method to remember short numbers like telephone numbers, Aadhaar card numbers, credit card numbers, etc. Use the Link Method or the Story Link Method to remember these numbers in their correct sequence.

- Use the Major System to convert long numbers into their peg letters. Chunk the letters to form words and sentences.

Remembering Addresses

- Use the Nickname Method to remember the name of the house, apartment and name of the road. Use any of the Number Systems to remember the door number or plot number.

Remembering Directions

- Peg each instruction or direction using the Number Shape System or the Number Rhyme System. Use Pure Links to associate each direction in their correct order.

Remembering Schedules and Appointments

- Use any of the Number Systems for the time of the appointment. Associate the time to the task at hand using either Pure Links or Story Links.

Remembering Birthdays, Anniversaries and Important Dates

- Use the Nickname Method to associate a person to his birthday or anniversary. Use the Number Shape Method or the Number Rhyme Method to remember the dates and the Major System to remember the year. Use peg words for each month.
- This method helps you remember past dates as well as future dates.

Remembering Names and Faces

- Use rhymes, familiar songs and personal meanings to remember names.

- Use the Nickname Method to associate the meaning of the names or the sound of the name with the person.
- Notice any distinguishing feature of the person's face and associate this with the sound or meaning of their name.
- Names can also be remembered by location and by using the Mental Snapshot Method.

Finding Lost Objects

- Be mindful of where you keep your things.
- Use the Mental Snapshot Method to remember where you keep something.
- Close your eyes and calmly visualize where you held the object last and work your way forward from there.

Remembering Dreams

- Use any of the memory systems to remember your dreams in order.

Chapter 9

The Amazing Power of Your Mind

'There is nothing either good or bad,
but thinking makes it so.'
—WILLIAM SHAKESPEARE, HAMLET

All of us hold internal conversations with ourselves as we go through our days. You may hear these conversations as a voice in your head holding a monologue, providing you with opinions and evaluations on what you are doing, as you are doing it. Sometimes, you may have a dialogue with this voice about something that you are anxious about or something that you are thinking of doing. If all this sounds a bit crazy, don't be alarmed. The voice or voices in your heads are nothing but your thoughts. The monologues and dialogues that you have with yourself is called self-talk.

You are who you are today because of the self-talk that constantly plays inside your head. Some of you may be more aware of your thoughts than others. If you haven't particularly been paying attention to your thoughts, now is a good time to start as these thoughts and what you say to yourself paves the way for your behaviour in situations. You may have positive self-talk which can be constructive and uplifting; or negative self-talk, which can be destructive and degrading.

The following story is an example of how positive and negative self-talk affects your outlook in life.

There was once a traveller who was walking from a village in the mountains to a village in the valley. As he walked along, he saw a monk working in a field, so he stopped and said to the monk, 'I'm on my way to the village in the valley, can you tell me what it's like?'

'Where have you come from?' enquired the monk.

The man responded, 'I have come from the village in the mountains.'

'What was that like?' the monk asked.

'Terrible!' the man exclaimed, 'no-one spoke my language, I had to sleep on a dirt floor in one of their houses, they fed me some sort of stew that had a yak or dog or both in it, and the weather was atrocious.'

'Then I think you will find that the village in the valley is much the same,' the monk noted.

A few hours later another traveller passed by and he said to the monk, 'I am on my way to the village in the valley, can you tell me what it's like?'

'Where have you come from?' enquired the monk.

'I have come from the village in the mountains.'

'And what was that like?'

'It was amazing!' the man replied, 'No one spoke my language so we had to communicate using our hands and facial expressions. I had to sleep on the dirt floor which was really cool as I've never done that before. They fed me some sort of weird stew and I have no idea what was in it but just to experience how the locals lived was great and the weather was freezing cold, which meant that I really got a taste of the local conditions. It was one of the best experiences of my life.'

'Then I think that you'll find that the village in the valley is much the same,' responded the monk.

From the story above, you can see how a positive outlook helps you enjoy what others may see as a dreary experience. This is why paying attention to your self-talk is very important as it can not only shape your moods but your actions as well. Since you are in your developmental years, your self-talk is very important as it may set the tone for the rest of your life. Your self-talk has the ability to either lower or strengthen your self-confidence, self-esteem and belief in yourself and the world around you. Now is the time to start respecting yourself and talking to yourself in a motivating fashion instead of putting yourself down or labelling yourself as fat, ugly, stupid, angry, selfish, rude, etc.

Observe if your thoughts are negative or positive. Observe situations that cause your thoughts to be negative. What are you saying to yourself in those situations? How do you feel? How do you react to situations that you perceive as negative?

This chapter focuses on identifying destructive self-talk and changing it to be more constructive and positive. The first step is to pay attention to your thoughts. The next step is to change negative thoughts into positive thoughts through affirmations. Once you are able to control your thoughts, you can manage distractions by clearing out mental clutter, practising mindfulness and managing mental stress.

Pay Attention to Your Thoughts

> 'Whether you think you can or you think
> you can't...you are right.'
> —HENRY FORD

Your thoughts are automatic. As described earlier in the free association exercise, certain words and events can trigger off a chain of associated thoughts effortlessly. For example, the word 'exam' can either have positive or negative associations for you depending on how you see it. If you did well in your last exam and your parents rewarded you for it, you may look forward to your upcoming exams. However, if you did not fare well and your parents punished you for it, you may be dreading the upcoming exams. In either case, the event of an upcoming exam is the same but how you look at it can differ.

How can your self-talk affect your life? Positive self-talk can motivate your behaviour and make you feel happy, but negative self-talk can demotivate you and make you feel horrible about yourself. Negative self-talk can even make you hate yourself. For example, say you answer a question wrong in class and your classmates laugh at you. If your self-talk is positive, you may feel a bit embarrassed but you may laugh along with your classmates thinking, 'At least I brought some laughter to this dull day!' On the other hand, if your self-talk is negative, you may feel extremely embarrassed and may think, 'I'm so stupid. How could I have made a silly mistake like that? Now everybody is laughing at me, I can't handle this!' Here, your negative self-talk affects your feelings.

The way that you talk to yourself can also lead to a certain kind of behaviour. For example, you may have got 55 per cent in an exam. What would your self-talk be? You may tell yourself that while these are not great marks, you will work harder on this subject and score better in your next exam. Since you think that you will work harder, you will make more of an effort in that subject to score better marks next time. However, if you tell yourself, 'I'm too stupid to get good marks. I'm a failure. I'll never pass,' you will be dejected and you will lose all motivation to study better next time. In the first instance, although you may feel sad about getting a low score, you still feel hopeful that you will do better next time. However, in the second instance, your thoughts of 'I'm too stupid. I will never pass…' blocks you from studying further and not only demotivates you but demoralizes you as well.

Do you see how your thoughts, feelings and behaviour are connected? This is why you need to be aware of your thinking pattern and observe if your natural way of thinking is positive or negative. If you find that your natural way of thinking is negative, you can work on changing it to something more acceptable and positive. The way to do this is through affirmations.

Pro Tips:

- Always talk positively to yourself about yourself. Be mindful of negative thoughts and see how to change them to more positive thoughts.

Affirmations

> *'Attract what you expect, reflect what you desire, become what you respect, and mirror what you admire.'*
> —JACQUELINE H. WALLER

In the previous section, you saw how positive thoughts lead to positive feelings and behaviour while negative thoughts lead to negative feelings and behaviour. In this section, you will see how to change negative thoughts to more acceptable positive thoughts with the hope that once your thoughts change, your feelings and behaviour will also change.

Let's continue with the previous example of your self-talk about exams. You may think—

'Oh no, not again!' which starts associated thoughts such as:

- 'What if I don't do well in this exam?'
- 'Will I get a rank this time?'
- 'My parents are going to start nagging me again.'

- 'There's so much to study in chemistry! How will I ever remember all the formulae?'
- 'Biology is so boring!'
- 'Anita has already started studying. She'll get better marks than me again.'

With these negative thoughts in mind, the behaviour that follows will be procrastinating studying and then finally trying to cram in the last minute. You may let yourself get distracted while studying, feel tired or sleepy every time you open your textbook and then panic at the last minute because you have not been able to complete your syllabus. This is all because of the initial negative thoughts that you had towards the upcoming exams.

How can you change this? You can do this through affirmations. Affirmations are positive statements that you make to yourself that then lead to positive attitudes, feelings and behaviour. It is, in essence, changing your negative thoughts into positive thoughts.

If you were to look at the very word 'exam' in a more positive way, some of the optimistic statements that you can make to yourself may be:

- 'Exams are challenging but I love challenges.'
- 'I have a good memory for what I study.'
- 'I find it easy to concentrate.'
- 'I remember everything that I study.'
- 'Learning formulae is fun!'

Some of these statements may not be true…yet. But if you repeat them to yourself often enough, you can change your thinking pattern into a more positive one and then these statements will come true. While making your affirmations, here are a few points to keep in mind.

Personal—Make sure that your statements are about you and not anyone else. Start each statement with 'I can…' or 'I have…' or 'I love…'

Example: Wrong—My parents will praise me for getting good marks.

Right—I enjoy getting good marks.

Positive—The words that you use in your affirmations are important. They need to be positive statements so that they will encourage you to fulfil them.

Example: Wrong—I will not get distracted while studying.

Right—I focus and concentrate well while studying.

Present Tense—Your affirmations must be worded as if they were true right now, even though you have not yet accomplished them.

Example: Wrong—I will become a more positive person.

Right—I am a positive and optimistic person.

Comparison-free—Focus only on yourself and what you can do. When you focus on what your classmates or friends are doing, you will always place them above you and put yourself down in the process. You do not need this kind of negativity in your life. This one takes a bit of practice but you can do it!

Example: Wrong—Anita will get better marks than me again.

Right—I am hard-working and am studying well.

Realistic—Your affirmations need to be realistic to some extent. If you have been failing all your subjects, you cannot expect to suddenly be your class topper (although it is definitely a possibility). While you do need to exaggerate your affirmations a bit, try and keep them within the realm of reality.

Example: Wrong—I am going to get 100 per cent in all my subjects.

Right—I am studying hard to get good marks.

Affirmations need to be repeated all the time. You can write them down and read them out aloud at every chance you get, or you can visualize them and mentally keep revising as often as possible. You can also make a poster or collage and hang them up near your bed so that they are the first things that you see when you wake up. Using words like quick, like, love, enjoy, fun, terrific, strong, etc. will give you more confidence.

Let's determine a few affirmations that would work for you. First, think of a problem area that you would like to change. Then follow it up with your affirmations.

Example:

1. Problem area—My marks need to improve.
    Affirmation—I am studying hard to get good marks.

2. Problem area—I need more confidence.
    Affirmation—I am full of confidence!

Try working out your own affirmations:

3. Problem area—I get stressed easily
    Affirmation _____

4. Problem area—I find studying chemistry very challenging.
    Affirmation _____

5. Problem area—I hate studying maths.
    Affirmation _____

6. Problem area—I find memorizing formulae difficult.
    Affirmation _____

7. Problem area—I never have time to exercise.
    Affirmation _____

8. Problem area—I can't do without junk food.
    Affirmation _____

9. Problem area—I go to sleep very late and wake up early for
    school and I'm tired all day.
    Affirmation _____

10. Problem area—I tend to complain a lot.
    Affirmation _____

Now write down your own problem areas and affirmations. At
the end, make a list of the affirmations and repeat it to yourself
everyday, as often as you can.

1. Problem area _____
    Affirmation _____

2. Problem area _____
    Affirmation _____

3. Problem area _____
    Affirmation _____

4. Problem area _____
    Affirmation _____

5. Problem area _____
    Affirmation _____

Now that you are more aware of your thoughts and have learnt
how to make them positive, you can manage thoughts that distract
you easily. For this, you need to be aware of your distractions
so that you can deal with them. You will be, in effect, throwing
out the mental clutter.

Pro Tips:

- Use positive affirmations on yourself.
- Even though it has not happened yet, talk to yourself as though you have already achieved your goal.
- Keep your affirmations personal, positive, in the present tense, comparison-free and realistic.

Throw Out the Mental Clutter

> 'When we throw out the physical clutter, we clear our
> minds. When we clear out the mental clutter,
> we clear our souls.'
> —GAIL BLANKE

You're studying for an exam but you keep having thoughts of 'I'm never going to finish studying on time', 'I'm going to flunk', 'If I don't get good grades, I will get punished at home.' Or you may be thinking of the person you have a crush on. Or you may be hungry while studying. Or your wrist might be aching from writing too much. Or you might have a headache. Or people around you are nagging you or putting pressure on you to study. Or... The list goes on.

You can find a million things to worry about while studying. While worrying about something or the other is normal, this is an added burden on you while you are studying. If you find yourself worrying about something while studying, write it down and then focus on your studies again. Writing down your distracting thoughts not only helps you realize what is bothering you but also helps you to deal with them when you can, probably at a later time. If the same concern keeps popping up, take the time needed to deal with it. Otherwise it will become a bigger issue that will distract you further from studying.

Examine your thoughts by asking yourself the following questions.

- Am I overreacting? Is it really that big a deal? Is it important in the long run?
- Am I jumping to conclusions?
- How accurate is this thought?
- Am I assuming or guessing how other people will react? Am I reacting based on those assumptions or guesses? Can I control what other people think or how they react?
- Am I labelling myself harshly? Do I really need to use extreme words such as 'stupid' or 'failure' or 'fat' to describe myself?
- Am I viewing one incident as either good or bad without considering that the reality may be in between?

If your answer to the above questions is 'yes', then the thoughts that are distracting you are actually unnecessary and useless. Try and look at your thoughts in a realistic way. If you find them to be unnecessary, useless or counterproductive, try and cut them out of your thinking process altogether. If you find them to be realistic, think of what you can do to deal with them.

You can also have 'worry time' if you can't stop worrying about something. Set aside about ten minutes every day and, just as you have a study space, assign yourself a 'worry space'. It could be a specific chair or any place in your house, like your terrace or living room. While you're there, think about all the things that are worrying you, but once you leave that place, make a conscious effort to put these worrying thoughts at the back of your mind so that you can focus on other things.

How can you focus? By being more mindful of where you are right now.

Pro Tips:

• While studying, if you find yourself worrying about something, write it down and keep studying so that you can deal with it later.

• If the same worries keep cropping up, take the time to deal with them and sort them out so that you can concentrate on your studies.

Mindfulness

> '*The clock's hand moves, but it is always now.*'
> —ECKHART TOLLE

Be here now. You can't re-do what has happened in the past and you do not know the future, so you might as well focus on what you are doing right now. When you are studying and you find your mind wandering, repeat this mantra to yourself—BE HERE NOW—and bring your focus back to your work.

Mindfulness is simply being aware of what you are doing right now, and shutting out all other distractions and thoughts. Through mindfulness, you will be able to hone your attention and concentration on what you are doing right now, for a longer period of time. Mindfulness also helps you maintain a good emotional and psychological balance. It improves your physical fitness, helps you remain grounded in the present and enjoy each moment as it happens. You will also be able to push past low moods, negative thoughts and low energy to get long-term results, simply by being more aware and focused on what you are doing right now and not what you could have done or can do in the future.

Mindfulness refers to being aware of the moment as it passes, without being judgemental about it. It helps you live peacefully in the moment without labelling it as good or bad. This allows you to dwell in the present and eliminate concerns, worry and anxiety related to your past or future.

Let's do a simple exercise to practise mindfulness. This practice aims to improve your thought process by helping you put aside distracting thoughts and focusing only on the task at hand; in this case, your studies.

1. Sit down comfortably on the floor, a chair or a cushion.
2. Close your eyes and press your tongue gently up to the roof of your mouth.
3. Inhale deeply till the count of four and let the air fill your abdomen. Hold your breath for seven counts and then breathe out through your mouth (your tongue should still be touching the roof of your mouth) for eight counts. Focus only on your breathing as you continue to breathe in and out.
4. Place your hand on your stomach while breathing. If your stomach is moving in and out, you are doing it right.
5. You might find your mind wandering. When you realize this, gently remind yourself to be here now.
6. After about four to six cycles of breathing in and out, bring your mind to your study material. Picture it in your mind so that you can ready yourself. Exclude all thoughts not connected to studying from your mind. See yourself sitting at the table and concentrating and studying. Focus only on what is to be learnt.
7. Now that you are more mindful of what needs to be learnt, open your eyes and begin studying.

This is a very simple exercise to keep you 'here and now'. Practise this exercise for ten minutes every day. You can increase this time to forty minutes a day, if time permits. You will soon find that your focus, attention and concentration have improved drastically. While studying, if you have any distracting thoughts, keep them aside and remind yourself—BE HERE NOW—and continue studying. Once you finish, you can allow yourself to think about the distracting thoughts.

If the distracting thoughts are stressful, you need to learn how to manage them so that you can concentrate better.

Pro Tips:

- Be here now. Live in the present moment knowing that you cannot change the past or predict the future.
- When you find yourself getting distracted, gently remind yourself to be here now and come back to the present and what you are currently doing.

Managing Stress to Concentrate Better

> *'Nothing can bring you peace but yourself.'*
> —Ralph Waldo Emerson

Stress is any mental or emotional strain that you might be going through. You may experience stress in the form of a younger sibling crying all the time, an older sibling talking on the phone or watching TV at a high volume, a parent nagging you to study, issues with classmates or teachers, a hectic tuition schedule or the fear of an upcoming exam. All these issues have the potential to distract you while you are studying.

It may help if you focus on and deal with the things that you can control and try to avoid or not worry about things that you cannot control. For example, while you cannot control what questions are asked in the exam, you can control the syllabus you study. Similarly, while soothing a younger sibling may not be in your control, asking an older sibling to reduce the volume of the TV or go to another room to talk on the phone may be within your control.

Physical and mental exercises, yoga and relaxation techniques may also help you reduce stress and increase concentration. Here are a few more tips.

- Set realistic expectations. You may not be able to study ten chapters in one day, but you may be able to study two chapters thoroughly. Know your limits.
- Take breaks throughout the day.
- Express your feelings instead of bottling them up.
- Have a healthy balance between studying, hobbies, friends and distractions.
- Focus on one task at a time, one subject at a time. Do not multitask.

You may tend to overthink, which causes you added stress. This happens when you are not aware of the destructive power of your negative self-talk and you do not know how to channel your negative thinking. Since you do not know this, the same negative thoughts trouble you over and over again and you may, therefore, overthink an otherwise simple situation.

For example, Harry needs to go to the airport to pick up his wife. He cannot decide whether to take the car or his bike. He thinks, 'If I take the car, I'll need to find parking and it's always difficult to find parking at the airport. If I take the bike, it will be easier to park but how will we lug two suitcases back? If I take the car, parking will be expensive. If I take the bike, parking is not so bad. It might be safer to take the car. If I take the bike, I will have an accident. Maybe I should take a cab. But what if I don't get a cab on my way back? No, I'll take the car. But what if I get stopped for speeding? I'll take the bike, but what if it starts raining?' You can see how one simple decision has led to such a long line of thinking. You can also see how this overthinking is stressing him out. Ultimately, the goal is to pick up his wife who has two suitcases, so the simplest solution would be to take the car.

When you think too much, your thoughts will automatically become negative and when your thoughts are negative, you inevitably begin to worry or become anxious. When you become anxious, you kill any kind of productive behaviour. This doesn't just happen in one situation but spreads to other situations as well and before you know it, you will be worrying about everything under the sun. Once this negative cycle begins, you will find that any little thing begins to stress you out.

You can combat stress by practising mindfulness and focussing on the 'here and now' rather than what has already happened or what you think is going to happen. Throw out the mental clutter by focussing on the things that you can control and forgetting about things that you cannot control. Stop overthinking. Be aware of your thoughts. If your thoughts are leaning towards negativity most of the time, use affirmations on yourself to change them to positive thoughts. Make sure that your behaviour changes according to your thoughts. Positive thoughts bring about positive feelings and behaviour which then bring about a positive lifestyle.

Pro Tips:

- Focus on things that you can control rather than worrying or getting upset and stressed with things that are beyond your control.
- Make sure you get enough physical and mental exercise.
- Set realistic expectations, take breaks through the day, express your feelings, have a healthy balance between studying, hobbies and friends.
- Stop multitasking and overthinking!

Have the Right Mindset

Whether you are in school or college, or you're working or retired, learning is something that happens throughout life. It is therefore important to have the right mindset so that you can be open to new learning. Your mindset can either help you grow or keep you stagnant depending on whether you have a growth mindset or a rigid mindset. If you have a rigid mindset, you close yourself off to learning anything new and may stay stuck in the same place indefinitely. If you have a growth mindset, you may show real desire to constantly learn and improve, not just in academics but in every area of your life.

Look at eighty-nine-year-old Grandma Josephine, for instance. She lives in a retirement home and all her children are abroad. About a year ago, her eldest son bought her an iPad and taught her how to use it. Whenever she forgets how to use a certain feature, she asks one of her nurses to teach her. She now video chats with her children and grandchildren almost every day, plays games on the iPad, reads e-books and uploads pictures of her garden on her Facebook page. She even watches her favourite movies on Netflix every now and then!

Seventy-year-old Grandma Phillis, on the other hand, who also lives in the same retirement home, has an iPad of her own but has not learnt how to use it. Instead, she complains that her children never keep in touch and even when they do, they call her on the phone only once a week. She also complains that she sees her children and grandchildren only once a year at Christmas when they are in India. Although her son had set up her Facebook account the previous year, she never logs on and does not keep in touch with her friends. She spends her days cribbing about the food and her children and grandchildren, and is mostly in a bad mood. She tends to sleep when she is not complaining.

Both grandmothers live in the same retirement home and

have no previous experience with computers or gadgets. Yet Grandma Josephine, at the ripe old age of eighty-nine, made an effort to learn how to use her iPad and has therefore been able to use it for various things, including keeping in touch with her family. Grandma Phillis, on the other hand, had written off technology and did not bother learning how to use the iPad. She was, therefore, not able to keep in touch with her family and resorted to complaining about them all the time.

As you can see, Grandma Josephine had a growth mindset, while Grandma Phillis had a rigid mindset. It is never too late to move from a rigid mindset to a growth mindset. Be like Grandma Josephine and keep your mind open to learning new things and developing new skills. Accept the fact that setbacks will happen but they can be dealt with and sorted out. Don't be afraid to ask for help.

Pro Tip:

- Always study with a growth mindset. Be enthusiastic about learning. This positive mindset is more than enough to motivate you to achieve new heights.

Pay Attention!

> *'Give whatever you are doing and whoever you are with the gift of your attention.'*
> —JIM ROHN

Do you remember how memory works? You first need to encode information, which is then stored for you to retrieve later. Encoding is the first step to memory and the first step to encoding is to pay attention to information. Attention is like a gate that lets in information experienced through the senses of touch, smell, taste, sight and sound. If this gate is closed, or even half-open, you literally would not register anything that you experience and therefore would not remember it at all.

The good news about attention is that it can be selective. While there are many distractions around you, you can choose what you want to focus your attention on and ignore the rest. Imagine having a conversation with your friend in a classroom full of students conversing loudly with each other. How would you be able to hear what your friend is telling you? Simply by tuning out all the other students in class and focusing on him. The same thing can be done with studies as well. There might be a number of distractions—your younger siblings might be fighting, the TV might be on, your neighbours might be playing loud music—but you would still be able to study by tuning out all the distractions and focusing only on your study material.

Another positive is that if you pay close attention to something that you are studying, you directly encode and store it in your long-term memory. Sometimes, you just need to glance through your notes and not really study them simply because you remember the lecture so well. This is because you paid close attention to the lecture and therefore you have already learnt your study material.

The bad news about attention is that it does not aid in repetition. This means that merely repeating your study material hundreds of times would be absolutely useless if you are not paying attention to it in the first place. Have you ever tried to memorize a list by repeating it over and over again only to forget it five minutes later? This is because while you think you are studying it by rote, if you didn't pay attention, it just will not 'stick' in your mind.

Pro Tips:

- Paying attention to what you are studying will go a long way in storing information in your long-term memory.

- You can also choose to pay attention to certain things while ignoring distractions.
- Merely repeating study material is useless unless you are paying attention to what you are reciting.

Take Interest!

> *'If you always do what interests you,*
> *at least one person is pleased.'*
> —KATHARINE HEPBURN

You generally pay more attention to things that you are interested in. Think about your favourite subject. You might find that you pay more attention to the lectures and notes in this subject than any other subject simply because it interests you so much. You may even be able to tune out all distractions and focus solely on the lecture and nothing else! Conversely, think about a subject that you find boring or that you do not enjoy. You might take double the time to study this subject and may not even pay attention to the lectures simply because you feel that it bores you to death! You might even struggle to study this subject simply because you are not motivated enough to study it.

Information that you find interesting is directly stored in short-term or long-term memory. A student, who may not be able to answer any questions in class, may be able to rattle off every single detail about the last cricket world cup—what the score was in which over, how much each batsman scored, etc.—simply because cricket is something that interests him and therefore he pays more attention to cricket matches than he does to his studies.

The most important thing about interest is that it can be created. You can actually develop interest in the subject that you find boring. Approach the subject with a growth mindset. Develop an interest in at least one aspect of the subject, even if it is only one chapter, and do further research on it. Use the memory techniques of association, visualization, imagination and location when you study this subject so that you can make it come alive through colourful pictures and ridiculous associations.

Pro Tips:

- You pay more attention to things that you are interested in.
- Interesting information is directly stored in your short-term or long-term memory.
- Interest can be created.

Manage Your Emotions

> 'Sometimes, memories sneak out of my eyes
> and roll down my cheeks.'
> —ANONYMOUS

Emotions are directly linked to memories. Certain memories that are vivid in your mind, like bringing a puppy home for the first time or the first time you saw your crush, have emotions attached to them. Because of this, every time you see a puppy or someone who resembles your crush, you may experience the same emotions that you felt all those years ago. Every time you have these memories, you may be reminded of the feelings that you experienced at that time as well.

People tend to pay more attention to things that they are emotional about. For example, if your favourite actor is in a new movie, you might pay special attention to every aspect about him (his haircut, physique, clothes, etc.) while watching the movie. Perhaps you will notice more details about the movie itself when watching it a second time simply because you overlooked them the first time. In the same way, a subject that excites you will elicit better attention than a subject that you find boring.

Your emotional state of mind has a direct impact on your attention. Whether it is a positive emotion like happiness, joy or excitement or a negative emotion like sadness, depression or anger, emotions obstruct your attention and block you from studying. This may happen because you might be so preoccupied with your thoughts that you get distracted from your study material.

You tend to notice things based on your mood as well. When you are happy, everything around you looks rosy and bright but when you are sad, you tend to notice every depressing thing around you. This is why it is important to regulate your emotions while studying. You can use your emotions to your benefit. Since everything looks rosy and bright when you are in a good mood, how about studying that difficult subject at that time? When your mood is low, how about studying your favourite subject? Do you think this might help?

Pro Tips:

- Emotions have a direct connection with memory and attention.
- You pay more attention to things that you are emotional about.
- Emotions can block concentration.
- Regulate your emotions and make them work for you.

Believe in Yourself

> *'Believe you can and you're halfway there.'*
> —THEODORE ROOSEVELT

Belief is nothing but faith. Have faith in yourself. Trust yourself. When you make your affirmations, say them with conviction.

You CAN do it! You ARE worth it! You ARE amazing! You ARE intelligent. You ARE very capable. You may think, 'But I've failed before. How can you ask me to believe that I will pass this time?' To that, I would say, 'I not only think that you will pass this time, but I think you will pass with good marks!' You don't have to believe me; you just have to believe in yourself. This may be easier said than done, but with the power of positive thinking, you will be able to concentrate and study and get the grades you want.

Pro Tip:

* Have faith in yourself and trust your abilities.

Exercise 1: Student Stress Profile[1]

Circle the answer that best describes you.		Strongly Agree	Mildly Agree	Mildly Disagree	Strongly Disagree
1.	I have trouble concentrating when I study.	4	3	2	1
2.	I get extremely nervous about tests.	4	3	2	1
3.	I often have headaches because of schoolwork.	4	3	2	1
4.	I have trouble sleeping before a big test.	4	3	2	1
5.	My heart races whenever I am called on in class.	4	3	2	1
6.	I am very concerned about what my friends think.	4	3	2	1

---

[1]Oeschsli, Matt, *Mind Power for Students*, St. Martin's Paperbacks, 1996.

7.	My parents are always putting pressure on me.	4	3	2	1
8.	I have trouble communicating with my parents.	4	3	2	1
9.	I worry a lot.	4	3	2	1
10.	I don't let people know how I really feel.	4	3	2	1

Maximum Score = 40   My Score = _____

Scoring:

40–36: Your stress levels are through the roof!

35–29: You better pay attention to your tension levels or you're headed for problems.

28–21: Average, but you can certainly improve how you deal with stress.

20–14: You are doing well.

13–10: You are amazing! You deal with stress very well.

Chapter 10

Tricks to Learning

Study in the Right Environment

Some people respond well in an environment that is soothing and calming but others may thrive in an environment that has a lot of hustle and bustle. Understanding the kind of environment you prefer is the first step to increase concentration while studying.

- **Ambience:** Make sure the room that you're studying in is well-ventilated and has good lighting. Often, when the light is dim, you strain your eyes more to see and therefore you expend more energy and get tired faster.
- **Reachable material:** Keep everything that is required at hand so that you do not need to get up to get anything. All notebooks, textbooks, pens and even water can be kept on the table or nearby. This saves you the trouble of getting up every time you need something and therefore helps you manage your time better.
- **Designated study area:** Don't study on your bed. Since your bed is associated with sleep, you will automatically feel sleepy or tired. Have a designated place in your house to study, preferably at a table, and use that space only to study. Just as your bed is associated with sleep, you can train yourself to associate your study area with studying. This will help get you into 'study-mode' much faster.
- **Be organized:** Keep your study space neat and organized,

with places to store your computer and books.

- **Posture:** Maintain the right posture when you study. Lounging on a bed or sofa while studying may make you feel sleepy. Hunching over your books will give you aches and pains, which will come in the way of studying.
- **Music:** Some people study better with background music, so it is okay to have it on low as long as it does not distract you from studying. Instrumental music works best.
- **Distractions:** Make it clear to your family that this is your study time and you should not be disturbed during this time. This includes having family members turn off the TV or watching it at low volume. You can ask them to use headphones while listening to music. You can also request them not to disturb you unless something is really important. All bathroom breaks, hunger pangs, etc. should be taken care of before study time as they have the tendency to interfere with concentration.

Eat Right

Eating healthy food has a direct link to better memory and concentration. Healthy food nourishes your brain while unhealthy food can make you sluggish and tired. Eating junk food, fried food and food rich in sugar such as sweets and ice creams make your mind restless and your body sluggish while food rich in proteins such as almonds, eggs and lean meat have the ability to raise your awareness and increase your concentration levels! Foods rich in glucose, vitamin B and iron boost oxygen levels in the brain, thereby raising alertness and increasing the power to recall information that was learnt.

People who have unhealthy eating habits or their diet in general is poor, face the risk of poor memory. People who go on crash diets or skip meals deprive their brain of much-needed nutrients and this may make them light-headed. You may have noticed that your concentration and focus suffers when you feel very hungry. Now imagine studying when you're feeling hungry and light-headed. Do you think you will be able to remember much?

Alcohol and smoking also have an adverse effect on memory. Alcohol causes vitamin deficiency which can further cause short-term memory loss. Cigarettes deposit tar in your lungs which can clog up arteries in your body, slowing down the blood flow to your brain. This can cause high blood pressure and increases the possibility of a stroke. Both alcohol and cigarettes are extremely toxic to the body and should be avoided completely.

Some foods that are good for the brain are:

- Beetroot
- Cherry tomatoes
- Green, leafy vegetables especially broccoli
- Fresh fruits, especially avocados, bananas and apples
- Nuts, especially almonds and walnuts
- Eggs
- Extra virgin olive cooking oil
- Fish—salmon, mackerel, tuna
- Turmeric
- Barley
- Berries
- Whole grains such as brown rice, rye bread, porridge, etc.
- Dark chocolate
- Green tea, chamomile tea
- Milk
- Herbs such as sage and rosemary

Foods that are bad for memory are:

- Spicy food
- Stale food
- Fried food
- Junk food such as burgers and pizzas
- Chocolates, sweets, pastries and ice cream
- Microwave popcorn
- Fruit juices
- Cheese
- Doughnuts
- Red meat
- Diet sodas
- Soy sauce
- Bacon and any other salted meats

I'm sure you must have a few favourites under the 'bad' category. You don't need to completely stop eating these foods but you can eat them in moderation. Try to avoid them as much as possible while studying, especially when exams are approaching.

Drink Water

Over 70 per cent of your body is composed of water and every function in the body is dependent on it, including the activities of the brain and nervous system. However, due to sweating, breathing and eliminating wastes from the body, you lose about 80 per cent of water from your body. When your body loses more water than you are replacing, dehydration kicks in and brain function is affected. It is therefore important to keep refilling your body with water.

Brain function depends on having an abundance of water. When your brain is working on a full reserve of water, you will be able to think faster, be more focused, and experience greater clarity and creativity. It is important to drink plenty of water throughout the day for optimal brain function because your brain does not have the ability to store water. Water gives the brain the electrical energy for all its functions, including thought and memory processes. Water is also needed for the brain's production of hormones and neurotransmitters. Nerve transmission requires half of the brain's energy. Drinking water just before or during a class may help to concentrate.

Exercise to Boost Your Brain

Any exercise that makes your heart rate increase such as aerobics, walking, jogging, swimming, climbing stairs, tennis, squash, badminton, dancing and Zumba improves your ability to think and is particularly good at enhancing memory. Exercise is also believed to encourage the growth of new brain cells in the hippocampus—an area of the brain important in memory and learning. In addition to this, exercise improves mood and sleep, and reduces stress and anxiety.

How much exercise is required to improve memory? A minimum of two hours of brisk walking or its equivalent per week is essential. Half an hour of moderate physical activity most days of the week, or 150 minutes a week would be even better.

Whatever exercise you choose, commit to establishing exercise as a habit.

Sleep Well, Study Better

Good sleep triggers changes in the brain that help new memories 'stick' better. This happens when connections between brain cells are strengthened by proper rest. As soon as you wake up, memory tasks can be performed more quickly.

It is okay to pull long hours when needed, but it is also important to get the sleep your body needs or all your efforts will be in vain. Keep in mind:

- Your body needs 7–8 hours of sleep each day.
- Studying when you are overly tired amounts to wasted time.
- Getting a good night's sleep will empower you with better concentration and retention skills.
- A power nap for twenty minutes after school or in the afternoon should also do the trick to increase concentration.
- Over-sleeping might make you lethargic and sluggish.
- Keep away all gadgets including your phone at least one and a half hours before going to bed as the light from the gadgets can over-stimulate your brain and make it hard for you to fall asleep.

Gadgets

Let's face it. Using gadgets while studying is a waste of your precious time. Incoming calls and the constant notification pings are also an added distraction and can break your concentration while studying. It is a good idea to keep your phone on silent mode or better still, in a different room for the duration of your study time. If you need to use a computer to study, make sure that it is used only for studying and nothing else. Declare your study space a gadget-free zone.

Multitasking

First, let's get this straight. There is no such thing as multitasking, only divided or selective attention. You may say, 'But…I'm good at multitasking! I can watch TV and do my homework at the same time and concentrate on both!' I would say no, that's not multitasking. You're just shifting your attention from one thing to another. Don't believe me? Let's take small tests and find out.

Test 1

Have a paper and pen/pencil ready. Now look at the following words and try to remember them. Take only thirty seconds to read and encode the following words. Once you are done, write them down. Ready? Start.

Paper	Magazine
Dog	Pineapple
School	Piano

Test 2

How did you do? Did you find it easy? Okay, now do the same thing, but this time, tap your right leg with your right hand the whole time while reading the following list. As before, take thirty seconds to read and encode them. Once you are done, write them down. Ready? Start.

Photo	Flying
Monkey	Pantry
Work	Burger

Test 3

Was it a tad bit harder to remember this time? Okay. Let's try this one last time. Read the following words while tapping your right leg with your right hand and at the same time, say 'BLA… BLA…BLA' loudly. Keep Bla-bla-ing and tapping while reading the words. Take thirty seconds. Ready? Start.

Kangaroo	Sweets

| Table | Piano |
| Fountain | Clouds |

Did you find this last test slightly more difficult than the previous two? Are you feeling a bit tired after this exercise? This is because when you divide your attention between two tasks, your brain finds it hard to encode everything at the same time and gets tired quickly. With the simple task, you were only asking your brain to read and remember one thing at a time. But as you went on with the tapping and then the bla-bla-ing, your brain had to do multiple things at once. As you can see, the number of words you recalled decreased with more distractions. If it didn't, well, kudos to you!

Your memory may in fact be excellent, but when your attention is divided among three or four things, your memory system can 'crash'. Memory processing involves encoding, storing and retrieval, which are easy to disrupt. This is why concentrating on one thing at a time when you study is important. If there are distractions in the environment that are beyond your control, your attention will get divided but it is possible to focus only on what is relevant and ignore what is not.

Fun! Fun! Fun!

Make learning as fun as possible. Try to play games using your subject material. Try to interact more with your study material rather than just reading it.

How can you make your study material more interesting and fun?

1. **Ask questions**—While studying, don't just swallow whatever is in your textbook. Ask yourself 'Why? When? Where? What? Who? And How?' questions. Once you have a fuller understanding of what you are studying, it

becomes easier to remember. You can also imagine that you are on a quiz show. Ask your sibling or a friend to ask you questions, giving you points or (fake) money for each answer!

2. **PQRST Method**—Preview—skim and scan the text to get the gist.

   Question—ask yourself questions about what you have read.

   Read—find the answers as you read carefully.

   Summarize—summarize what you read in your own words

   Test—test yourself on what you have studied.

3. **Play games**—Play games with your study material. If you need to draw a diagram in biology, look at it for about a minute, then close the book and see if you can reproduce it. The focus is on interacting with what you have just learnt.

4. **Timer**—Have a timer that goes off every twenty-five minutes. Challenge yourself to study and concentrate as much as possible during that time.

5. **Be creative**—Try to use your imagination as much as possible while studying, as demonstrated earlier. Your creativity and imagination can be as wild as possible and can make even the dullest facts appear fascinating. Use all your senses to see, hear and feel your study material. Try and make the image as funny or as rude as possible. You can even use symbols in your visualizations. Once you have visualized a certain study material, don't forget to revise and rehearse.

6. **Music**—If it does not distract you, listen to soft music, preferably instrumental music to help you study better. Sometimes, putting your study material to music can

also be fun. Do you need to memorize a poem? Why not make it a song. Need to memorize dates? Why not put it to music. For example, 'On 15 August 1947, India reached Independence heaven.' Can you make this into a simple tune?

7. **Breaks**—You know that old saying, right? 'All work and no play makes Jack a dull boy.' Make time for play as well, however, make sure that your leisure activities do not distract you from studying. For example, you may want to check Facebook during your ten-minute break, but the next time you look up from your phone, you might realize that you've actually wasted more than twenty minutes browsing through your timeline!

8. **New Skills**—Take time to study something new or practise something that you have already learnt. Whether it is playing a musical instrument, learning embroidery or learning to cook something new, the skills you learn along the way also help hone your attention and you will find focusing on your studies much easier.

9. **Accents and voices**—Try reading something that you think is boring with a funny accent or a goofy voice.

10. **Posters**—Make small posters of your study material that you can hang up around your room.

11. **Rewards**—Reward yourself for completing something that you found particularly tough. Treat yourself to an ice cream or that much-awaited TV episode. Go on, you've earned it!

Exercise 1: Recipe—Memory Smoothie

Here's the recipe for the ultimate memory boosting drink. This delicious drink will help to stabilize blood sugar, increase blood flow to the brain and supply your body and brain with nutrients.

120ml unsweetened carrot juice	3 ice cubes
75g frozen or fresh blueberries	71g toasted almonds or walnuts
75g peeled and grated raw beetroot	½ teaspoon fresh lime juice
40g chopped avocados	1 thin slice fresh ginger

Place all the ingredients in a blender and blend until the texture is smooth and velvety.

Exercise 2: Brain Games—Multiplication Tables—Buzz! Fizz! Duck!

Have you ever had to sit and mug up your multiplication tables? Well, here's a fun game to learn and remember them. You need two or more people to play this. Let's start with 3 times tables.

Sit in a circle with your friends and begin counting in sequence from the number one. Each player shouts out one number when it's his turn. If a multiple of 3 comes up, don't say the number, just shout 'Buzz!' Any number that has a 3 in it is also 'Buzzed'. For example, 13 and 23 are also 'Buzzed'. When you come to 31, you need to say buzz one, buzz two, buzz buzz (because there are two 3's in 33), buzz four, etc.

Example—1, 2, Buzz, 4, 5, Buzz, 7, 8, Buzz, etc.

Want to make the game tougher? Add in multiples of 7 and call it 'Fizz'. So, all multiples of 3 are Buzz, all multiples of 7 are Fizz. Since the number 21 is a multiple of both, you need to shout 'Buzz! Fizz!'

Want to make it even tougher? Add in multiples of 8 and call it 'Duck!'

Example—1, 2, Buzz, 4, 5, Buzz, Fizz, Duck, Buzz, 10, 11, Buzz, Buzz (13 has a 3), Fizz, etc.

Remember, any number that has a 3, 7 or 8 is also buzzed, fizzed or ducked respectively (for example, 27, 37, 38, etc.). The game is fast-paced. Any player who skips a Buzz, Fizz, or Duck, or who takes too long to answer is out. You can make up a fun punishment for these players. Count till 100. If you want to make the game even tougher, once you reach 100, start counting backwards to 1.

Exercise 3: Brain Games—Solar System Crossword Puzzle

Crossword puzzles are a great way to keep your mind active and focused. Try practising more difficult crossword puzzles. You can find them in daily newspapers. One you have mastered it, graduate to cryptic puzzles.

Read the clues given below and write down the answers in the corresponding boxes. The answers are at the end of the chapter.

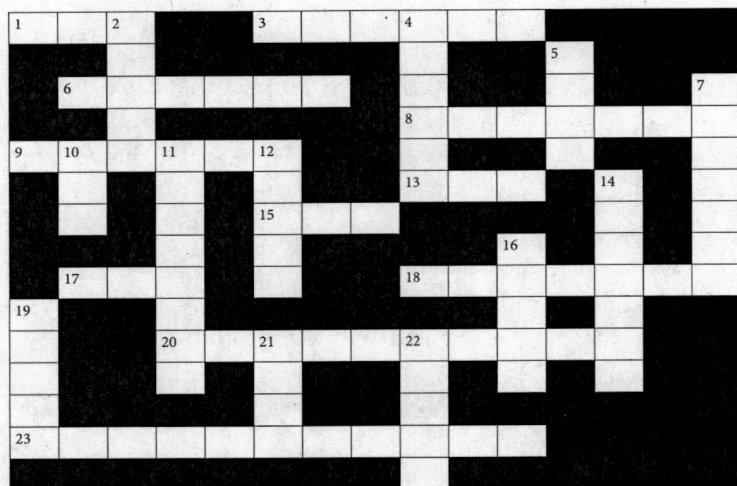

Across

1. The sun is made of hot _____.
3. Planet named after the Roman god of agriculture.
6. Large star system.
8. Planet furthest away from the sun.
9. Of the universe.
13. Closest star to the Earth.
15. Earth's residents collectively called.
17. Venus is hot and _____ (opposite of wet).
18. Force that keeps a planet moving in orbit.
20. Layer of gas that surrounds a planet.
23. Consists of a star and planets orbiting it.

Down

2. Luminous objects in the night sky.
4. Third largest planet in our solar system.
5. The sun _____ in the west.
7. Planet closest to the sun.
10. The Earth has only _____ moon.
11. Our solar system is part of this galaxy.
12. Celestial body that has a tail.
14. Largest planet in our solar system.
16. Covers 70 per cent of Earth's surface.
19. Planet named after the Roman goddess of love and beauty.
21. Nicknamed 'The Red Planet'.
22. Now called a dwarf planet.

Answers

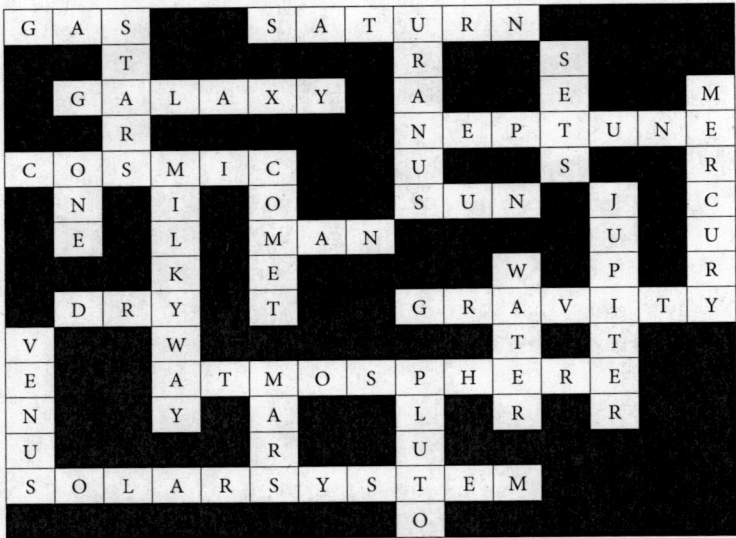

SUMMARY

- Make sure your environment is conducive to studying.
- Eat healthy. Drink lots of water.
- Exercise well.
- Sleep well.
- Keep gadgets away while studying.
- Do not multitask while studying.
- Studying need not be drudgery. Have fun!

Chapter 11

50 Memory Tips

Here are a few memory tips in addition to what has already been described in this book. Some of these may sound a bit quirky and strange but they help to boost memory. Just try them and see!

1. **Fish tank**—Have a fish tank in the room where you study. This has a calming effect on the mind and will decrease your anxiety while increasing your concentration skills.

2. **Keep a pet**—Studies show that having pets such as dogs, cats, turtles, hamsters, etc. can help keep your mind calm and enhance your memory. Just make sure that the care and upkeep of your pet does not come in the way of your studies.

3. **Make your bed**—As soon as you wake up, fold your blanket and straighten out your bedsheet and pillows. Hey, you've accomplished your first task of the day! Although this is a small task, it will motivate you to accomplish more throughout your day.

4. **Say no to cigarettes, alcohol and drugs**—While cigarettes, alcohol and drugs may give you an initial boost, they decrease your memory substantially.

5. **Chew gum**—Studies have shown that chewing gum while studying helps you encode new information faster and improves your long-term memory.

6. **Eat your favourite food often**—Eating your favourite food gives you a sense of happiness and satisfaction as it helps release the good hormones in your body. Beware not to eat

too many sweets, though!

7. **Write with your non-dominant hand**—Practise writing with your 'other' hand. If you are right-handed, write with your left hand. If you are left-handed, write with your right hand. This will help to strengthen your brain and give you more brain power.

8. **Learn something new every day**—Try and learn something new every day, whether it is a fact, a new word, a bit of trivia, a new skill, etc. This helps keep your mind sharp.

9. **Learn to play a musical instrument**—Learning to play a musical instrument increases the capacity of your memory, refines your time management and organizational skills, teaches you perseverance, enhances your coordination, improves your mathematical ability, reading and comprehension skills, sharpens your concentration, boosts your listening skills and teaches you discipline.

10. **Be creative**—Plan activities with your family and friends to enhance your creativity. You can plan a scavenger hunt and write down clues for your family or friends to follow, have a costume party but use only clothes that you already have (don't buy ready-made costumes), and instead of buying presents for friends' birthdays, try making something yourself—like a glass painting.

11. **DIY projects**—Try a few Do-It-Yourself (DIY) projects such as setting up a balcony garden from scratch; knitting, embroidery, quilling or crochet projects; papier-mâché or woodwork projects, etc. Doing all these things will hone your motor movements and power of concentration. They also help to ward off depression and lighten your mood, thereby protecting your brain from aging.

12. **Solve problems**—Don't focus on just maths problems. Often, playing strategy games such as chess, Chinese checkers and

Scrabble also help hone your problem-solving and analytical skills which are needed for maths. Try doing daily crossword puzzles and Sudoku in the newspaper.

13. **Learn a new language**—Learning a new language will strengthen the executive functioning of your brain, which increases your focus and concentration and improves memory.

14. **Reduce screen time**—Screen time is time spent in front of the TV, computer, smartphone, tablet, etc. Studies have shown that too much screen time leads to obesity, attention problems, sleep disorders and problems at school. While it is common to binge watch your favourite TV shows, try to resist this urge. Pace yourself. Watch one episode per day. Reduce the time that you spend watching programs. For teenagers and adults, the recommended screen time is not more than two hours a day.

15. **Reduce social media usage**—Limit your time spent on Facebook, Twitter, Instagram and other social media. Scrolling through your Facebook or Twitter timeline is equivalent to multitasking since each post on your wall is completely different and drags your attention in different directions. For example, on Facebook, one post may be political while the next might be a recipe for tandoori chicken. The post after that may be a friend's holiday pictures, followed by a meme about something or the other. In four posts, your mind has been dragged in four different directions. Notifications on phones are like drugs—Facebook 'likes' and Twitter 'favourites'—can keep you addicted to these apps as they give you a high. Try to limit your social media to not more than half an hour a day. This half hour is included in the two hours that you get for screen time per day.

16. **Movie technique**—When studying, try to visualize your

study material like a movie that's playing inside your mind. You can use an existing movie if it helps and simply replace the characters and objects with what you are studying. See the movie vividly in your mind. Make it as colourful as possible with clear audio and movements. This will help it stand out in your mind.

17. **Read more**—Developing the habit of reading regularly will help you retain the information better. Reading is a much better neurological challenge for your brain than watching a TV show or a movie. Read fiction and non-fiction. Don't just stick to your area of interest; try and read random articles as well. Reading random informative articles, either in newspapers or magazines improves your vocabulary, expands your general knowledge, gives you an entirely new perspective of the world and of course, enhances your memory.

18. **Physical exercise**—Physical exercise not only keeps your body in shape but strengthens your mind as well. A quick exercise of just twenty minutes is enough to boost the oxygen levels in your brain and positively affects the growth of brain cells. Exercising in the mornings is especially beneficial as it gives you a jump start to your day and a sense of accomplishment even before your school or work day begins.

19. **Sleep**—Too little sleep can make you feel stressed and worried and can lead to emotional problems such as anger, anxiety, depression, etc. Have a proper sleep schedule. Don't drink caffeinated drinks after 5 p.m.—this includes coffee, tea and any aerated soft drink.

20. **Treatment**—If you feel depressed or too anxious, meet a doctor for medication or a psychologist for counselling. Depression causes mild to severe memory loss while anxiety makes it difficult to concentrate and form new memories. Do not self-medicate.

21. **Spend time with friends**—People who are socially active have a healthier brain. Spending time with friends is also a good way of keeping depression at bay. Surround yourself with good people, interact with them and stay connected. This can act as a mood booster and can bring positivity to your life.

22. **Meditate**—Meditating for even a few minutes a day can relax your brain, make you feel calmer, enhance your ability to think clearly, increase blood flow to all parts of your brain and improve your memory.

23. **Laugh**—Laughter really is the best medicine for your brain as it releases good hormones in your body and prevents stress hormones from taking over. Laughter helps to normalize your blood pressure and puts you in a good mood, which further enhances the health of your brain. Spend time with fun people. Don't take yourself too seriously—learn to laugh at yourself when you make a mistake rather than beat yourself up over it.

24. **Sing**—Music itself is great for memory, for, when you sing, you not only need to learn the lyrics but the tune as well. This can stimulate your brain and enhance your auditory memory.

25. **Guess ingredients**—Since your memory is strongly connected to your sense of smell, this is a fun way to test it. Try and guess the ingredients of food that you are eating, just by tasting it. This not only tests your sense of taste but increases your concentration as well. This also helps you eat mindfully.

26. **Perfumes**—Your sense of smell can be a powerful memory aid. Use a particular perfume or cologne when you study. On the day of the exam, use the same perfume or cologne. While writing your exam, the smell of the perfume or cologne may bring back memories of when you were studying the

information in the first place! You can use different perfumes while studying different subjects and wear the corresponding perfume for the corresponding exam.

27. **Write**—It doesn't matter what you write about, just write! Use a pen or pencil and avoid typing on keyboards. This enhances your processing abilities and increases your learning capabilities and motor skills thereby sharpening your brain.

28. **Teach**—No, you don't have to go to a school or college to teach students. If you are able to explain a lesson the way your teacher would, you will be able to gauge how much you have understood. This will help you cement the material in your memory. You can either teach a pretend audience or you can explain your study material to friends or family members. Encourage them to ask you questions. This will help you understand your study material from a different perspective and will also improve your analytical skills.

29. **Explain to a five-year-old**—My statistics professor always made us explain college-level statistics to her as though she were a five-year-old child. This helped us break down complex statistics into a much simpler, easy-to-remember form and enabled us to understand it better in the long run.

30. **Tell yourself stories**—Narrating events to yourself as they are happening or making events into stories stimulates your creative abilities and enhances your power of observation. You will also create a more convincing framework inside your mind and add context to what you are currently thinking, feeling or studying. Imagine this—your exams are looming and your parents have started nagging you to study. While you may find the nagging stressful, there's nothing you can do to stop it. Instead, imagine this in the context of a comedy sitcom on TV. How would the storyline go? Don't you think that making this stressful situation into a comedy story may

help alleviate your stress?

31. **Gaming**—Yes! Games such as Grand Theft Auto and Need for Speed have many positive effects on the functioning of your brain. These games are expansive in terms of maps, missions, objectives, etc. and this requires your brain to adapt to more complex ways of thinking. These games also help with problem-solving and analytical skills and help in reinforcing long-term memory. Having said that, as mentioned before, don't spend too much time on gadgets but limit your game-play. Remember, all screen time needs to amount to not more than two hours per day (when exams are far away).

32. **Jigsaw puzzles**—Assemble jigsaw puzzles. No, they are not just for little kids. Try and find a 500-piece or a 1,000-piece puzzle. Puzzles are a good way to increase your perception, observation, reasoning abilities and analytical skills. They also help you increase your concentration. Try not to do jigsaw puzzles online. When you have the puzzle in hand and you can work out how to fit the pieces together, you will also enhance your kinaesthetic learning abilities.

33. **Rubik's cube**—Working out a Rubik's cube has the ability to stimulate multiple parts of your brain which other games cannot do. Working out a Rubik's cube helps develop your spatial intelligence and enhances your kinaesthetic and visual encoding skills.

34. **I went to the moon…**—Here's a game to learn long lists. Play this with two or more people. The first person starts, 'I went to the moon and all I took with me was a hammer.' The next person continues, 'I went to the moon and all I took with me was a hammer and an egg.' The third person continues, 'I went to the moon and all I took with me was a hammer, an egg and a tortoise'…and so on. This helps you remember long lists effortlessly. See how many words you can

remember in the correct order. Use the location technique or any of the number systems to remember the order of the list.

35. **Magic Crystal Ball**—Just as a magic crystal ball may tell you your future, imagine looking into one and see yourself finishing a particular chapter. Feel how happy and relieved you will be. Now keeping this end goal in sight, start studying. This is nothing but setting a short-term goal for yourself and envisioning it happening. Once you are able to envision it, you will be motivated to start the process of completing it!

36. **Walk backwards**—Why follow the same pattern you've been following throughout your life? Walk backwards. Try walking up- and downstairs backwards (but be careful!). This actually exposes your brain to new levels of planning and analysing.

37. **Word play**—Try and make puns during conversations with friends. While puns are funny and clever, they also help your brain think out-of-the-box and look for new connections in words or phrases. For example:

a) What's the worst thing about planning a party in space? You have to planet!

b) Yesterday, a clown held the door open for me. I thought it was a nice jester!

c) How do you make antifreeze? Steal her blanket!

d) It was an emotional wedding. Even the cake was in tiers!

e) What does a house wear? Address!

38. **Solve riddles**—Riddles are fun and sometimes absolutely ridiculous. Solving riddles not only activates your brain and makes you think creatively, but also triggers one of the key memory principles of imagination. For example, you are in a room with no doors, windows, or any exit. The only items in the room are a mirror and a table. How do you escape?

Answer: Look in the mirror, then at the wall and back at the mirror to see what you saw. Use the saw to cut the table in half and join the two halves to make a whole. Put the 'hole' on the wall and climb out. Lame, right? But as ridiculous as the answer is, I bet you will be able to remember it for a long time to come! Also, since the answer is completely out-of-the-box, you will need to suspend traditional logic and think creatively.

39. **Reverse letters**—Try and recite the letters of the alphabet in reverse order every day. This will push you out of your usual comfort zone and exert greater pressure on your brain to think. Reversing letters helps stimulate your brain and improves your thinking abilities while increasing your concentration.

40. **Recite numbers**—Try reciting series of numbers to yourself. This can be odd numbers, even numbers, counting in fives or tens, multiplication tables, palindromes, value of pi to the 100th decimal, etc. Start with simple number series and move to complex numbers later. This improves your mathematical as well as your analytical skills.

41. **Draw**—You don't have to be a great artist. Just draw. Draw anything that you like. See the image clearly in your mind and try to reproduce it on paper or on the computer. The left hemisphere of the brain is said to process information in a more verbal analytical way while the right hemisphere is more visual and intuitive. Since you tend to use the left hemisphere more when you study, an activity like drawing can stimulate the right hemisphere and create a better image in your memory. When both hemispheres are in use, you tend to learn better and expand your memory.

42. **Different fonts**—When studying something on your computer, use different fonts for different parts of your study

material. Switching to a different font gives your brain a sudden jolt and stimulates it. When writing, use different colours or different fonts for headings and subheadings. For example, if you write your main headings in print, write the information in the subheadings in cursive writing. Information under the main heading and subheadings can be written down in different colours.

43. **Create flashcards**—Flashcards are small pieces of paper that have key points written on them. Instead of carrying heavy books around, you can just revise your lessons by looking at your flashcards. You can draw mind maps on them or just use them to list key points. Either way, they are a great device to aid memory.

44. **Connect the dots**—Identify something on the left side of your field of vision and something on your right side. Move your eyes back and forth between the two. This helps stimulate both hemispheres of the brain which helps in better memory.

45. **Breathe**—Studies have shown that when you breathe through your left nostril, you activate the right hemisphere of your brain and make it more dominant. The same is true when you breathe only from your right nostril—you activate the left hemisphere of your brain. Breathing from the left nostril calms you down and helps you sleep better. Breathing from the right nostril gives you more energy, helps you stay alert, and enhances clarity of thought.

46. **Yoga**—Practising yoga exercises helps you focus and increases concentration and awareness. Start your day with the Surya Namaskar asanas. Try to do as many as you can.

47. **Finish what you start**—Completing activities, chores or projects gives you a sense of satisfaction and closure. If you do not complete something, it may work on your mind and cause anxiety. Don't do many things at the same time. Focus

on one thing and finish it.

48. **Tune out to tune in**—When you are studying, any noise or movement can be a distraction. Learn to tune out distractions that you have no control over such as blaring loudspeakers, the sound of traffic or the neighbour's loud TV. Focus and concentrate on what you are studying instead. Once you begin to concentrate, you will automatically tune out everything else.

49. **Change location**—While it is recommended that you use the same location to study all your subjects, sometimes, switching locations may also help as it generates new associations in your brain and makes it easier to remember facts later.

50. **Observe**—Remember you will recall only what you observe and pay attention to, so it will help if you hone your powers of observation. Watch the world closely, form connections between what's happening and what you know. The more you see, the more accurate your memory will be!

Appendix

Workbook

Using any of the memory techniques or a combination of memory techniques, try to work out the following exercises.

Exercise 1: Observation Exercise—Bus

You are driving a bus which contains fifty people. The bus makes one stop and ten people get off, while three people get on. At the next stop, seven people get off, and two people get on. There are two more stops at which four passengers get off each time and three fares get on at one stop and none get on at the other. At this point, the bus has to stop because of mechanical trouble. Some of the passengers are in a hurry and decide to walk. So, eight people get off the bus. When the mechanical trouble is taken care of, the bus goes to the last stop where the rest of the people get off.

Now, cover the paragraph above and without re-reading, answer the following questions.

1. How many stops did the bus make altogether?
2. What is the name of the bus driver?

Exercise 2: Visualization Exercise

You can enhance your visualization skills by practising the following steps on any random object in your house. This exercise will not only hone your powers of visualization, but will improve your observation skills as well.

1. Take any household object. It can be something as mundane as a spoon or a water bottle. Assuming you choose a spoon, study it for about 15–20 seconds to observe as many aspects of it as possible.
2. Now close your eyes and recall as much about the spoon as possible. Try to see it in your mind. To begin with, all you may be able to recall is the general shape of the spoon or its coloured handle. When you have run out of ideas, open your eyes and take in more detail, such as any engraving or maybe the manufacturer's name.
3. Close your eyes once more and add your new observations to the original mental picture. Then open your eyes again to observe more detail. Keep repeating this pattern of open eyes—observe—close eyes—recall, until you have absorbed as many features of the spoon as possible.
4. Now, without looking at the spoon, try to draw it, using the mental image that you have of it. The drawing does not need to be perfect; it just needs to have all the elements that you have observed about the spoon in it.

Try this exercise every day with a different object. You will soon find your powers of visualization and observation improving for everything around you. Remember, observation is the first step to encoding any kind of information if you would like to recall later.

Exercise 3: Imagination Exercise

You've come to school and you realize that you have not done your homework. Your teacher asks you to explain yourself. Think of five possible reasons why you could not do your homework. Make them as imaginative and ridiculous as possible. As you know, sometimes fact is stranger than fiction. As outrageous as your excuses are, they need to be plausible. Can you do it?

Exercise 4: Mindfulness Exercise—5 Senses Drill

1. Pause what you are doing for a moment and take one or two deep breaths to help bring you into the present moment.
2. Look around you, and silently name three things that you see in your immediate vicinity.
3. Now listening to the sounds around you, silently note and name three things that you can hear right now.
4. Bringing your attention to your body, silently name three sensations that you can feel in this moment (like warmth, tingling, contraction, coolness...)
5. Bringing your attention to smell and taste, what do you notice in your immediate awareness when you bring your attention to these senses—name what you experience.
6. Take one or two breaths to finish this mindfulness exercise.

Exercise 5: Acrostics

Using acrostics, memorize the following formulae of physics.

1. Linear momentum $\mathbf{p} = \mathbf{mv}$, where p is the product, m is the mass and v is the velocity.
2. Angular momentum $\mathbf{L} = \mathbf{I\omega}$, where L is the angular momentum, I is the momentum of inertia and ω is the angular velocity.
3. Ohm's Law $\mathbf{V} = \mathbf{IR}$, where V is the voltage, I is the current and R is the resistance.
4. $\mathbf{W} = \mathbf{mg}$, where W is weight, m is the mass and g is gravity.
5. $\mathbf{E} = \mathbf{mc}^2$, where E is energy, m is mass and c^2 is the speed of light squared.

Exercise 6: The Number Phrase Technique

Using the Number Phrase Technique, memorize the following numbers.

1. Your bank account number—392234
2. Your ATM pin number—2839
3. Your cycle lock combination—48372
4. Your licence plate number—6239
5. Your friend's apartment number—5134

Exercise 7: Mental Snapshot Method

Using the mental snapshot method, take a snapshot of the formula for compound interest. Look at the formula. Observe every letter, number and sign. Observe the shape that the formula makes. Close your eyes and see the image clearly in your mind. Now close this book and write down the formula from memory.

$$A = P \left(1 + \frac{r}{n}\right)^{nt}$$

Where A = amount accumulated
P = principal amount
r = annual interest rate
n = compounds per period
t = number of periods

Exercise 8: Pure Link System

Using the Pure Link System memorize the following list of thirty words in the correct sequence. Challenge yourself by adding more words to this list.

duck, vase, bulb, roof, fish, cupboard, salt, pin, handbag, mirror, foot, carpet, door, pepper, horse, egg, cow, beetroot, soil, cake, moon, heart, hula

hoop, donkey, money, foreign,
glove, biryani, tent, ghost.

Exercise 9: Story Link System

Using the Story Link System memorize the following list of thirty words.

nest, toe, hospital, plant, dog, pipes, straws,
notes, eclipse, memory, dwarf, ice cream, t-shirt,
books, roses, wand, sword, comb, glass, snow, clouds,
screwdriver, ears, apples, magic, love, song, frog,
chariot, shampoo.

Exercise 10: The Number Shape System—Gandhi–Irwin Pact.

Using the Number Shape System, learn the terms of the Gandhi–Irwin Pact:

1. Withdraw all ordinances and end prosecutions.
2. Release all political prisoners except those guilty of violence.
3. Permit peaceful picketing of liquor and foreign clothes shops.
4. Restore the confiscated properties of the Satyagrahis.
5. Permit the collection and manufacture of salt by persons near the sea coast.

Exercise 11: The Number Rhyme System—Classification of Soil

Use the Number Rhyme System to learn the classification of soil. You can also use nicknames to break up the different types of soil (alluvial = all + you + whale).

1. Bun—Alluvial Soil
2. Shoe—Black Soil (Regur)
3. Tree—Red Soil
4. Door—Laterite Soil
5. Hive—Arid and Desert Soil
6. Sticks—Forest and Hill Soil
7. Heaven—Peaty and Marshy Soil
8. Gate—Saline and Alkaline Soil

Exercise 12: Mind Maps—Methods of Irrigation

Read the following extract about methods of irrigation in India and draw a mind map for it. Remember to break down the information into keywords or phrases.

There are four methods of irrigation—wells, canals, tanks and the modern method of sprinklers and drip system. Well and canal irrigation are most important and widespread.

1. Well Irrigation—Wells are used extensively in Uttar Pradesh, Punjab, Bihar and Haryana. They have been introduced in Gujarat, Telangana, Andhra Pradesh, Maharashtra, Rajasthan, West Bengal and Madhya Pradesh. Wells may be of three types—unlined wells, lined wells and tube-wells.

    a) Unlined Wells (kuchha wells)—These wells are dug by the farmer near his field. These wells can be constructed where the water table is high, and are not lined with bricks or stones and are easier and cheaper to dig.

    b) Lined Wells (pucca wells)—These wells are lined with bricks or stones. These wells are perennial and are constructed where the water table is high and more or less permanent and the ground is made up of soft rocks to facilitate digging and drilling. It is more expensive to construct.

c) Tube Wells—A tube well is a very deep hole bored into the ground with a drilling machine and the water is pumped out with the help of electricity. Tube wells can irrigate larger areas than surface wells and are more reliable during periods of droughts since they are very deep and reach the zone of permanent saturation of the water table.

2. Canal Irrigation—This is one of the most important methods of irrigation as it irrigates over 40 per cent of the total irrigated area. Canal irrigation is more widespread in northern India where the rivers are perennial. The water from these rivers are stored in reservoirs by building dams across the rivers. The water is then distributed to the fields through a network of canals and distributaries. There are two types of canals—perennial canals and inundation canals.

a) Perennial Canals—Canals which flow throughout the year are called perennial canals. They draw their water from perennial rivers or artificial lakes made by the construction of a dam or a barrage which maintains a high level of water on the upstream side. Hence the canal can draw water throughout the year and irrigate large areas. Such canals are common in northern India where most of the rivers are perennial.

b) Inundation Canals—These canals are taken out of rivers without building barrages, dams or weirs at their head to regulate the flow of water. When the river is flooded, the excess water flows into these canals. While these canals are useful for controlling floods, they are not very useful for irrigation during the drier months or in areas where rainfall is uncertain.

3. Tank Irrigation—Tanks are constructed by building earthen or masonry walls across a valley or depression, behind which rainwater collects. This water is then used during the dry months. It is important that the ground is made up of non-porous rocks to prevent loss of water through seepage into the ground. In India, about 12 per cent of total irrigated area is irrigated through tanks. They are more prevalent in Tamil Nadu, Andhra Pradesh, Karnataka, Odisha, Maharashtra, West Bengal, Rajasthan, Madhya Pradesh, Bihar and Kerala. This kind of irrigation is found more in the Deccan Plateau, and the reasons for that are:

- The terrain of the Deccan Plateau is very uneven with many natural depressions where tanks can be built.
- A large area of the Deccan Plateau has hard rock underground.
- Tanks also help in raising the water table, thus making more water available in wells.
- Tanks are easier and cheaper to build.

4. Modern Method—The modern method compensates disadvantages of traditional methods and thus helps in the proper way of water usage. The modern method involves two systems: Sprinkler system and Drip system.

   a) Sprinkler System—A sprinkler system as its name suggests sprinkles water over the crop and helps in an even distribution of water. This method is more advisable in areas facing water scarcity. Here a pump is connected to pipes which generate pressure and water is sprinkled through nozzles of these pipes.

b) Drip system—The water supply is done drop by drop straight at the roots using a hose or pipe. This method can also be used in regions where water availability is less.

Exercise 13: Mind Maps—Geography—Mineral Resources of India

Work out a mind map of the Mineral Resources of India. Only the uses and areas of manufacture of the metals, non-metallic and energy minerals are discussed below but you can add further details such as by-products, refinery locations, sites of deposit, sites of coal mines, etc. You can colour code each metallic or non-metallic mineral as a whole or you can colour code by uses and manufacture sites. To remember the cities of manufacture, you can use any of the memory techniques for long lists such as location (route journey technique) or the alphabet technique. You can also look at a map of India and mark off where iron ore, manganese, etc. are produced. This will give you a good visual to work with.

Main Central Image: Mineral Resources of India

First Subheading: Three main classifications—1. Metallic Minerals, 2. Non-Metallic Minerals, 3. Energy Minerals

1. Metallic Minerals

a) Iron Ore—Uses: Manufacture of iron and steel
Produced in Odisha (Keonjhar, Mayurbhanj, Bonai areas)
Jharkhand (Singhbhum and Palamau Districts)
Chattisgarh (Durg and Bastar Districts)
Maharasthra (Chandrapur, Ratnagiri and Sindhudurg)
Telangana and Andhra Pradesh (Guntur)

Tamil Nadu (Salem and Tiruchirapalli)
Karnataka (Shimoga, Bellary, Chitradurga, Chikmaglur)
Goa

b) Manganese—Uses: Manufacture of good quality steel (makes steel tough, no rust)
Produced in Madhya Pradesh (Chhindware and Balaghat Districts)
Odisha (Keonjhar, Mayurbhanj, Talcher, Sundergarh Districts)
Karnataka (Shimoga, Chitradurga, Bellary, North Kanara, Tumkur, Belgaum, Dharwar)
Maharashtra (Nagpur, Bhandara)
Andhra Pradesh (Srikakulam)
Telangana (Nizamabad)
Jharkhand (Chaibasa, Palamau, Singhbhum)
Rajasthan (Banswara)

c) Bauxite—Uses: Manufacture of aluminium
Produced in Madhya Pradesh (Amarkantak plateau, Maikal hills, Balaghat)
Chhattisgarh (Bilaspur)
Jharkhand (Ranchi, Palamau)
Gujarat (Jamnagar, Surat)
Maharashtra (Kolhapur, Ratnagiri)
Karnataka (Belgaum)
Tamil Nadu (Nilgiri, Salem, Coimbatore)
Goa

2. Non-Metallic Minerals
Limestone—Uses: Cement industry, as Flux in Iron and Steel industry, in paper, glass, fertilizers and chemical

(caustic soda, soda ash) industry.

Produced mainly in Madhya Pradesh (Jabalpur, Satna, Rewa)

Maharashtra (Chandrapur, Nanded)

Tamil Nadu (Salem, Madhurai, Ramnathpuram)

Odisha (Birmitrapur, Sundergarh)

Karnataka (Shimoga, Gulbarga, Bijapur)

3. Energy Minerals

   a) Coal—Uses: Commercial energy, manufacture iron and steel, chemicals, paints, etc.

      Produced in Jharkhand (Jharia, Bokaro, Girish, Karanpura, Ramgarh)

      West Bengal (Raniganj Coalfield)

      Madhya Pradesh (Mohpani, Singrauli, Sohagpur)

      Chhattisgarh (Korba)

      Maharashtra (Pench-Kanhara, Nagpur, Chandrapur)

      Tamil Nadu (Neyveli)

      Telangana (Singareni)

      Gujarat (Umarsar)

   b) Petroleum—Uses: Fuel

      Produced in Assam (Digboi, Naharkatiya, Rurasagar, Nunmati)

      Gujarat (Cambay Basin, Ankleshwar, Koyali, Kalol, Navgaon)

      Off-shore Mumbai (Mumbai High, Bassein, Aliabet)

Exercise 14: Room Journey Method

Using any of the journey methods, memorize the information in Exercise 12 on Irrigation in India. With the Room Journey Method, you can use four rooms since there are four main points (wells, canals, tanks and modern method). In each room, peg objects with each sub-point under each main heading. For example, you will place Point 1—Well Irrigation—in your first room. Since this has three points under it—Unlined Wells, Lined Wells and Tube Wells, you will need to peg three objects in your first room to these points. Remember to break up the information into key points or phrases so that you can place each key point or phrase at a particular location or peg it to a particular object in a room.

Exercise 15: Route Journey Method

Using the Route Journey Methods, try to remember your chores for today.

1. Fill up petrol in bike.
2. Buy snacks.
3. Water the plants.
4. Pick up laundry.
5. Clean your room.
6. Call technician to fix the microwave.
7. Call and wish a friend on his birthday.
8. Go to a friend's house to collect history notes.
9. Withdraw money from the ATM.
10. Pay tuition fees.

Exercise 16: The Major System

Using the Major System, convert the following numbers into words and the words into numbers.

1. Dazzle	—	_____	1. 101	—	_____
2. Nomad	—	_____	2. 125	—	_____
3. Antique	—	_____	3. 123	—	_____

4. Molehill	—	_____	4. 454	—	_____
5. Unshaved	—	_____	5. 409	—	_____
6. Males	—	_____	6. 61	—	_____
7. Recall	—	_____	7. 580	—	_____
8. Magic	—	_____	8. 507	—	_____
9. Rarely	—	_____	9. 704	—	_____
10. Rainbow	—	_____	10. 714	—	_____
11. Chitchat	—	_____	11. 890	—	_____
12. Canopy	—	_____	12. 836	—	_____
13. Economy	—	_____	13. 979	—	_____
14. Fashion	—	_____	14. 901	—	_____
15. Buffoon	—	_____	15. 1000	—	_____

Exercise 17—Combination of Techniques

Using the Number Shape Method, the Number Rhyme Method, the Major System, the Nickname Method and the pegs for months, memorize the first twelve prime ministers of India along with the date that they took office.

Hint: Since all of them are in the 1900s, you can disregard the first two digits of the year—19—and convert only the last two digits using the Major System. You can use any of the number systems to convert the dates.

1. Jawaharlal Nehru—15 August 1947
   Nickname _____
   Conversion–Date _____
   Month _____
   Year _____
   Story Link _____

2. Gulzarilal Nanda (acting)—27 May 1964

Nickname _____

Conversion–Date _____

Month _____

Year _____

Story Link _____

3. Lal Bahadur Shastri—9 June 1964

Nickname _____

Conversion–Date _____

Month _____

Year _____

Story Link _____

4. Gulzarilal Nanda (acting)—11 January 1966

Nickname _____

Conversion–Date _____

Month _____

Year _____

Story Link _____

5. Indira Gandhi—24 January 1966

Nickname _____

Conversion–Date _____

Month _____

Year _____

Story Link _____

6. Moraji Desai—24 March 1977

Nickname _____

Conversion–Date _____

Month _____

Year _____

Story Link _____

7. Charan Singh—28 July 1979
   Nickname _____
   Conversion–Date _____
   Month _____
   Year _____
   Story Link _____

8. Indira Gandhi—14 January 1980
   Nickname _____
   Conversion–Date _____
   Month _____
   Year _____
   Story Link _____

9. Rajiv Gandhi—31 October 1984
   Nickname _____
   Conversion–Date _____
   Month _____
   Year _____
   Story Link _____

10. V.P. Singh—2 December 1989
    Nickname _____
    Conversion–Date _____
    Month _____
    Year _____
    Story Link _____

11. Chandra Shekhar—10 November 1990
    Nickname _____
    Conversion–Date _____
    Month _____
    Year _____
    Story Link _____

12. P.V. Narasimha Rao—21 June 1991
    Nickname _____
    Conversion–Date _____
    Month _____
    Year _____
    Story Link _____

Exercise 18: Nickname Method

Using the Nickname Method, link the following derived quantities and base quantities to their units and symbols.

Derived Quantity	Unit	Symbol	Nickname	Association
Force	Newton	N		
Pressure	Pascal	Pa		
Energy, Work	Joule	J		
Power	Watt	W		
Frequency	Hertz	Hz		
Electric charge	Coulomb	C		
Electric resistance	Ohm	Ω		
Electromotive force	Volt	V		
Velocity	Metre per second	m/s		

Base Quantity	Unit	Symbol	Nickname	Association
Length	Metre	M		
Mass	Kilogram	Kg		
Time	Second	S		
Electric current	Ampere	A		
Temperature	Kelvin	K		
Intensity of light	Candela	Cd		
Amount of substance	Mole	Mol		

Exercise 19: Brain Games—Word Scramble

Unscramble the following words.

Hint: They are all insects.

NAST	AYGPRNI NMATSI	CLIE
LEEBET	GIWAERS	IDPRSES
YLF	PSESHRAGPOR	EIRETTM
OOCHCRKAC	EBES	RIEKCTC
LNFOAYGRD	ALFE	ITKSC GBU
OUTMQISO	MHTO	ELYFSRHO
BTLTEUYFR	CCIDAA	PAWS
AGDBLYU		

Exercise 20: Brain Games Rigmarole

This is a fun memory game for two or more players. Players must count from one to ten, calling out three-word phrases that start with the same letter as the corresponding number. For example, player one starts with 'one' and she can say 'one opens oranges'. Player two then repeats the first phrase and adds her own phrase for 'two', which could be 'two tiny toes'. Player three repeats what player one and two have already said and continues with a three-word phrase for 'three'. The game continues till ten and starts over at one again. At this point, players need to remember the first ten phrases when they restart with 'one'. A player who cannot remember a previous phrase or cannot add a phrase is out of the game.

Exercise 21: Brain Games—Total Recall

This is a fun observation game that you can play with two or more friends. You will need a tray and a towel that can completely cover it, 20–30 small objects, paper and pens. Place the small objects on the tray and cover them with the towel. The objects can be anything—fruits, small toys, coins, jewellery, etc. The tray is prepared before the game begins. Give each player a paper and pen.

Uncover the tray for one minute and ask each player to merely observe and memorize the objects on it. Cover the tray after a minute and ask each player to write down the objects that they can recall. They are given two minutes to write everything down.

The winner of the game is the player who gets the maximum number of items correct. If two or more players have written down the same number of items, the player who has described the item more accurately wins. For example, if there is a one-rupee coin on the tray, the player who writes down 'one-rupee coin' wins over the player who has simply written 'coin'.

Exercise 22: Brain Games—20 Questions

This is a guessing game for two or more players. Player one thinks of a person, place or thing. The other players have to guess who, where or what it is by asking twenty questions. The player who guesses correctly wins. If players are unable to guess within twenty questions, player one wins. Note, the questions need to be yes or no questions. Player one cannot be asked to describe or say anything more about what he is but can answer only with a 'yes' or a 'no'.

Exercise 23: Brain Games—Word Association Game

This is a game of imagination where you need to think of logical or ridiculous associations between words. If it is ridiculous, there needs to be a plausible explanation for the associations.

This game is for two or more players. Player one starts by saying any random word that comes to mind and player two has to quickly say a word that is associated with it. For example, if player one says 'garden', player two may say 'flower'. Player three then has to say another word that is associated with 'flower'. If he has heard it as 'flour' he can then say 'baking' which is acceptable as it is a plausible association even though player two meant it as 'flower'. Try and make the associations as ridiculous as possible, but there needs to be some logical connection between the words, no matter how slim. For example, player one may say 'purse' and player two may then say 'cow!' If he can explain the logic behind his association—that the purse is made of leather and leather comes from cows, the word is accepted. If there is no logical explanation or if the explanation is not unanimously accepted by the other players, the player is out of the game.

Exercise 24: Brain Games—Sudoku

The classic Sudoku game consists of a grid of eighty-one squares. The grid is divided into nine blocks, each containing nine squares. The rules of the game are simple: each of the nine blocks has to contain all the numbers 1–9 within its squares. Each number can only appear once in a row, column or box. The difficulty lies in that each vertical nine-square column, or horizontal nine-square row across, within the larger square, must also contain the numbers 1–9, without repetition or omission. Every puzzle has just one correct solution.

Fill the grid so that every row, every column and every 3x3 box contains the numbers 1–9.

Sudoku—Beginner's Level

				9	8	7	6	
	3	9	7					5
	6							4
	7					8		3
3			4	8	9			2
2		8					1	
6							9	
5					1	4	2	
	2	1	9	4				

Sudoku—Difficult Level

		4	7					9
	5			4			8	
9						7		
5					6			
	8			5			9	
			4					6
		3						4
	2			7			5	
1				8	6			

Exercise 25: Brain Games—Word Search

The following grid contains the names of thirty birds. Try and find them. The words can be horizontal (forwards and backwards), vertical (top to bottom and bottom to top) and diagonal.

heron, pheasant, flamingos, ducks, goose,
swan, sparrow, pelicans, falcon, egret, starling,
thrush, bittern, kingfisher, cuckoo, crow, broadbills,
weaver, pitta, quails, stork, owls, hawks, toucans, eagles,
ravens, kites, grebes, crossbill, parrots.

C	R	O	S	S	B	I	L	L	W	Z	S	D	E	Z	B	A	N	S	S
I	H	S	U	R	H	T	Q	U	W	O	O	D	P	E	C	K	E	R	S
M	N	P	X	L	S	Q	D	B	D	T	R	K	K	Z	I	A	V	K	T
Q	W	A	M	V	B	I	T	T	E	R	N	C	B	T	S	S	A	I	A
E	M	R	B	R	O	A	D	B	I	L	L	S	E	M	F	T	R	N	R
A	P	R	F	H	G	B	P	Q	S	U	P	S	Z	L	B	O	Q	G	L
G	O	O	S	E	P	V	J	Y	E	S	E	D	A	G	Z	R	W	F	I
L	W	W	P	G	D	S	K	D	B	I	L	M	U	V	Q	R	X	I	N
E	G	D	E	R	M	R	Q	E	E	V	I	I	D	S	S	A	Z	S	G
S	G	Z	E	E	O	P	F	Y	R	N	C	B	O	T	Y	P	S	H	A
S	D	E	S	T	M	H	E	R	G	Y	A	D	S	W	E	A	V	E	R
N	L	K	S	C	H	E	R	O	N	V	N	J	U	T	W	A	B	R	T
A	C	Z	T	Y	D	A	S	S	E	W	S	K	C	U	D	F	D	S	B
C	D	S	F	D	F	S	K	L	B	K	I	W	X	O	O	K	C	U	C
U	M	P	I	T	T	A	A	A	W	D	E	F	A	V	G	D	R	T	S
O	F	A	L	C	O	N	D	A	B	O	V	A	D	N	G	D	G	W	F
T	K	R	D	S	D	T	H	F	S	O	G	S	L	I	A	U	Q	E	H

ANSWERS

Exercise 1: Observation Exercise—Bus

1. 5 stops
2. Read the first word of the paragraph. YOU are the bus driver. Therefore, your name is the name of the bus driver.

Exercise 16: The Major System (possible answers)

1.	105	1.	Dust
2.	231	2.	Downhill
3.	217	3.	Denim
4.	355	4.	Roller
5.	268	5.	Rasp
6.	350	6.	Cheat
7.	475	7.	Leaves

8. 367		8.	Lasik
9. 445		9.	Kisser
10. 429		10.	Guitar
11. 616		11.	Fibs
12. 729		12.	Female
13. 723		13.	Back up
14. 862		14.	Pasta
15. 982		15.	Tease sauce

Exercise 19: Brain Games—Word Scramble

ANTS	PRAYING MANTIS	LICE
BEETLE	EARWIGS	SPIDERS
FLY	GRASSHOPPER	TERMITE
COCKROACH	BEES	CRICKET
DRAGONFLY	FLEA	STICK BUG
MOSQUITO	MOTH	HORSEFLY
BUTTERFLY	CICADA	WASP
LADYBUG		

Exercise 24: Brain Games—Sudoku

Sudoku—Beginner's Level

4	5	2	3	9	8	7	6	1
1	3	9	7	6	4	2	8	5
8	6	7	1	2	5	9	3	4
9	7	5	6	1	2	8	4	3
3	1	6	4	8	9	5	7	2
2	4	8	5	3	7	6	1	9
6	8	4	2	5	3	1	9	7
5	9	3	8	7	1	4	2	6
7	2	1	9	4	6	3	5	8

Sudoku—Difficult Level

8	1	4	7	2	5	3	6	9
3	5	7	6	4	9	1	8	2
9	6	2	8	1	3	7	4	5
5	3	1	2	9	6	4	7	8
4	8	6	3	5	7	2	9	1
2	7	9	4	8	1	5	3	6
7	9	3	5	6	2	8	1	4
6	2	8	1	7	4	9	5	3
1	4	5	9	3	8	6	2	7

Exercise 25: Brain Games—Word Search

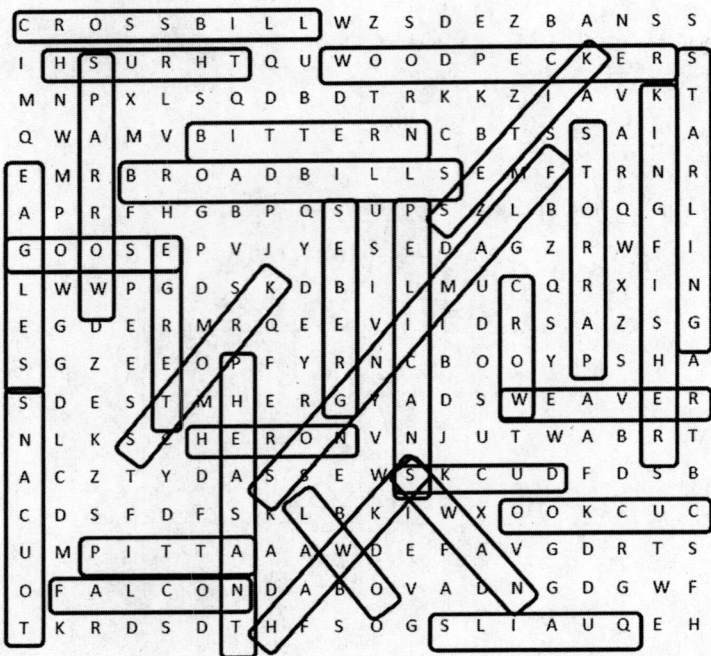

```
C R O S S B I L L L W Z S D E Z B A N S S
I H S U R H T Q U W O O D P E C K E R S
M N P X L S Q D B D T R K K Z I A V K T
Q W A M V B I T T E R N C B T S S A I A
E M R B R O A D B I L L S E M F T R N R
A P R F H G B P Q S U P S Z L B O Q G L
G O O S E P V J Y E S E D A G Z R W F I
L W W P G D S K D B I L M U C Q R X I N
E G D E R M R Q E E V I D R S A Z S G A
S G Z E E O P F Y R N C B O O Y P S H A
S D E S T M H E R G A D S W E A V E R
N L K S Z H E R O V N J U T W A B R T
A C Z T Y D A S E W S K C U D F D S B
C D S F D F S K L B K I W X O O K C U C
U M P I T T A A W D E F A V G D R T S
O F A L C O N D A B O V A D N G D G W F
T K R D S D T H F S O G S L I A U Q E H
```

References

Baddeley, A. (1996). *Your Memory A User's Guide.* London: Prion.

Brennan, H. (1997). *Change Your Way of Thinking.* London: Scholastic Children's Books.

Buzan, T. (2010). *The Memory Book* . Harlow: BBC.

Chambers, P. (2017). *How to Train Your Memory.* London: Bluebird.

Chowdhury, N.R. (2015). *A Step-by-Step Guide to a Smarter Memory.* New Delhi: Rupa Publications India Pvt. Ltd.

Devi, S. (2011). *Super Memory: It Can Be Yours!* New Delhi: Orient Publishing.

Kapadia, M. (2000). *Increasing Memory Power.* Mumbai: Shree Book Centre.

Lorayne, H. (2015). *The Complete Guide to Memory Mastery.* Mumbai: Jaico Publishing House.

O'Brien, D. (2011). *How to Pass Exams.* New Delhi: Viva Books Private Limited.

Oechsli, M. (2000). *Mind Power for Students.* Mumbai: Magna Publishing Co. Ltd.

Poddar, T. (2015). *Smart Memory Techniques to Improve Memory.* New Delhi: Pustak Mahal.

Powell, M. (2015). *Memory Power.* Bath: Parragon Books Ltd.

Singhal, A.S. (2015). *How to Memorize Anything.* Gurgaon: Random House India.

Standard X Text Books

Kundra, D. (2016). *I.C.S.E. History & Civics Part II for Class X.* New Delhi: Goyal Brothers Prakashan.

Rajen, R. (2016). *A Textbook of Geography Class X* (23 ed.). Mumbai: Apt Printers & Publishers Pvt. Ltd.

Singh, S. (2016). *Concise Chemistry Class X.* New Delhi: Selina Publishers.

Acknowledgements

I would like to thank Rupa Publications, especially Yamini Chowdhury, for this wonderful opportunity to write this book. A very special thanks to Ritabrata Joardar for his beautiful illustrations. A BIG thank you to my parents Mr and Mrs Solomon, my husband Rabin Stephen and my daughters Shifrah and Annika for their support and patience during the writing process. Thank you!